# MICROSCOPY OF NUMEROLOGY

## Numerology Simplified

### Know About Your Self
### Through Numerology

## Baldev Bhatia

PARTRIDGE
A Penguin Random House Company

**To order additional copies of this book, contact**
Partridge India
000 800 10062 62
orders.india@partridgepublishing.com

www.partridgepublishing.com/india

# With the blessing of GOD GANESHA

# WITH THE BLESSINGS OF GOD SHIVA

## "OM NAMAH SHIVAY"

# OMKAR

# ABOUT NUMEROLOGY

Numerology is a wonderful Science OF NUMBERS. It is a cosmic Science, which reveals, the hidden mysteries of numbers. Its origin can be traced to earlier times, when a person first began to identify various causes, in his immediate behavior, environment, and his nature of controlling over his temperament.

Research and deep studies done in the past have revealed that every number has a different characteristic and has different occult significance with very specific power. This power of difference n numbers has reflected not only a distinctive character on the basis of their qualities, with the cosmic force, and influencing the laws of nature by governing them in different ways.

The commencement begins with NUMBER ONE, indicating a powerful dynamic force, and great abilities over everything.

These are followed by number 2, 3, 4 and 0. This zero number has not been assigned any distinct role, but in association with other numbers it does play an important part. As anything multiplied by zero becomes zero.

There are various types of numbers. These are called Birth Numbers (the prime number), the LUCKY Numbers, the Year Numbers and the Name Numbers. As such there are also the House Numbers, the Vehicle numbers, your Telephone Numbers etc.

Now these different numbers of an individual when vibrates and influences well, life becomes much more interesting and fruitful for the person.

Name number is the number obtained from the addition of all the alphabets in our name, which is further divided into various other types of numbers such as, Personality Number and Destiny Number and Ambition Number.

Number 7 are great visualizers, thinkers and philosophers. Number 9 is highly suitable for politics as it confers qualities of aggressive approach dynamism, and good organization capacity. It often makes them courageous and fearless.

Though number 9 natives tend to face difficulties and hassles initially but later on, by their own persistent and hard work, they can ensure success and often hit the target and become head-liners.

Numbers 1 and 9 are more stable, strong than number 7. People with number 7 are more comfortable with regards to their religion and their religious and spiritual matter and have the capability of preserving and strengthening their cultural heritage, but on the face of it, this number is full of uncertainties, tribulations, dirty and foul play.

Whereas, number 7 is good on the spiritual world, number 9 happens to be a top number on the materialistic world and is good for great success on the political front.

Number 9 has qualities of diplomacy, tact, ability to take the masses which is inbuilt in them, among the weaker sections of society. Number 9 people feel restless when their leadership is questioned but once their leadership is well established, they march easily to their road to victory.

When any one changes his name, a grand new set of cosmic vibrations start influencing his luck and fortune. These have tremendous impact on all aspects of his life. Whereas it is often said, that when a lady changes, her first name, after her marriage her style life and fortune too takes a new turn.

In many circumstances and communities, when a man is suffering and is not in perfect health or is ill and is not good at responding to treatment, he is advised to change his name and that is changed for his speedy recovery and with this the new vibrations are set in him to respond to a more positive and fast manner.

Thus by correcting the alphabets in your name number balances in your name vibrations, thus giving you the strength to derive maximum benefit from this Science of Numbers.

It is also advisable to look at the both the basic number and the horoscope before deciding as to which name number would vibrate better for you.

Similarly, by changing the name of a house, street or a city, the general fortunes of these places undergo changes.

Numerology in simple words deals with the prediction of the future with the help of numbers. It takes care of the basic desire of almost all human beings and peeps into the future. It deals with the practical application of the primary laws of mathematics to the material existence of a native.

This science deals with the nine major planets—Sun, Moon, Jupiter, Uranus, Mercury, Venus, Neptune, Saturn and Mars with their characteristic features. Each one of these nine planets is associated and assigned to a number ranging from 1 to 9, depending on which planet carries the tendency to vibrate to a certain number.

These nine planets, with each different number influence the human life in an important and substantial way. The planetary positions at the time of a person's birth ascertain the personality of that individual in correspondence to their prime number. A primary and a secondary planet governing each individual at the time of birth respond to their own number or their birth number.

Hence, after the birth, the individual starts responding to the vibrations of that number or the planet by which he is governed.

All the characteristics of this native, ranging from his emotions, thinking, reasoning, desires, health, career, are all governed by these numbers with their corresponding planets.

Now when this number is in similarity or harmony with the prime or birth number of any other person, he experiences a better understanding and relationship with that person.

According to the theory of numerological only a name and its birth number rule a person. He would face grand opportunities and severe difficulties in life in accordance to the influence of numbers manipulating in his lives.

The most common form of Numerology often called as the "Western Form of Numerology", or the "Pythagorean System", is considered to be the most popular, enduring and simplified system of all. It is a self-help method ever created.

Even the Greek, Hebrews, Chinese, Japanese, Egyptians, and early Christians, all practiced this number system to gain a deeper understanding of themselves, the other individual and the universe.

Pythagorean Numerology or the Pythagoras system was brought into practice by Greek philosopher and mathematician called Pythagoras, who combined this mathematical science of various alphabets into numbers.

Presently its popularity continues to grow, and Numerology columns appear regularly in leading newspapers magazines and fancy literature.

More and more Numerologists are consulted regularly for almost everything from personal problems to romance, to business. As the growing world becomes more powerful and computerized and is largely dependent on numerical systems, the fascination with this ancient spiritual science grows quite rapidly.

Numbers are the universal means of understanding and communication with each other. And while languages vary from culture to culture, the meaning of numbers do specify the meaning of words.

In Numerology, each letter is associated or assigned with a number, and each number carries its own distinct personality. Hence, the numbers associated with any word can convey deep messages to all, without having any communication with them.

Numerology is the study of numbers, or the art of numbers and the manner in which they reflect certain aptitudes and character tend to speak of each letter. Each letter has a numeric value that provides a related cosmic vibration.

The sum of the numbers in your birth date and the sum of value derived from the letters in the name provide an power of vibrations.

These numbers show a great deal about character tics, purpose of life, which motivates, as to where the talents may lie. Experts in numerology use the numbers to determine the best time for major events, actions, positive moves and movement in life.

Numerology on the other is often used as a useful tool to decide our important decisions as when to invest, marry, travel, change jobs, and when to relocate or when to change our residence and premises.

How does numerology work is still a mysterious question. Is is an occult study, or Is it a cosmic force Do numbers have vibrations effects or is it a God's gift to humanity is still to be discovered in depth. Therefore an attempt has been made to make this cosmic science of number simplify in a easy manner for beginners.

Pythagoras, a Greek mathematician is said by many to be the originator, of numbers, and the Father of Numerology. The actual origins of numerology is said to be pre-dated of Pythagoras, the most common and popular being the very old the "Hebrew Kabbalah".

This mystic power of numbers became the source of wealth of literature in the coming decades and Indeed, it has moved very rapidly which was aloof from most learned scholars in the past.

# INTRODUCTION

Numerology attempts to explain us the basics of this interesting cosmic science. It teaches us how to change the letters in our name to numbers which reveal much about our personalities and potentials.

It's best to first learn numerology keywords as "BIRTH NUMBER, LUCKY NUMBER and these provide us a quick understanding of numerology and its general influences on our heavenly bodies. Moving into the basic numbers, we will quickly learn the basic number is first and most important number.

Numerology of your name provides an array of your expression and character tic of your number and is often called your birth number and the sum total of your birth date is the destiny number or your lucky number. Once again the names varies from person to person and the numbers carries different meaning and characters of these names.

Numerology's foremost and the main purpose is to gain a better understanding of who are and what we are, what we are made of, and what is the future that is stored for us.

This science enables us to determine key points in our lives, and the time and moments in which to make our major moves action and decisions, such as undertaking a journey traveling, investing and marring, all through the manipulation and calculations of numbers related to us.

The most important aspect of Numerology is determining your goal and path, which involves adding up the sum digits of your birth date.

Numerology offers a reliable and profound method of examining our inner nature and to understand the physical, spiritual and psychological processes that form our life actions and solid experience.

The science provides deep understand the insights of what makes an excellent method of guiding the streams of our daily lives.

No matter what are one's goals in life, with the help of Numerology it can be reached with without much delay and with lesser difficulty.

Numerology helps the native to learn how he should emphasize his power and strength as well as overcome his weaknesses, by providing almost the knowledge he needs to know from these vibrational forces and the cycles that are defined.

Through these insights, one gains more understanding about oneself and the others, which will help in dealing with others.

Numerology also in acts emotional interactions, building our strengths, helping us to clear the obstacles, and with the help of these numbers, we are able to see the trends of events that will happen in any particular time of the year, month or a day.

Using this combination of numerology and self-improvement teachings, one is able to help thousands of people realize their true potential and dreams with their actions with their aim of meeting the target.

Numerology is the science of numbers. It gives the study and opportunities that you may encounter in your lifetime. It is a tool that provides self-help and meaningful advice for all types of situations.

For knowing your numerological readings you have to know first your Lucky Number. Write down your date of birth first. Then add all the numbers in it. You will arrive at a sum. Then add the numbers in that sum number. That is how you will have your Lucky Number.

For Example:

If you are born on 29-10-1977 here is the way to find your lucky number. Add all the numbers in the birth date 2+9+1+0+1+9+7+7=36.

36 is the sum number.
Add the numbers in it.3+6=9 is your Lucky Number.
Secrets of your name

Now if you don't know your date of birth, you can still find out your lucky number from your name itself. And for this, you need to use Pythagoras Method. In this method every letter is assigned a number as per the following table.

First write down the numbers from one to nine

On a piece of paper than place the English

ALPHEBETS just below each number as shown in the example below:

| 1 | 2 | 3 | 4 | 5 | 6 | 7 | 8 | 9 |
|---|---|---|---|---|---|---|---|---|
| A | B | C | D | E | F | G | H | I |
| J | K | L | M | N | O | P | Q | R |
| S | T | U | V | W | X | Y | Z |   |

Find out your lucky number by writing down your name first. Than arrange or assign the number to every letter in your name. Add all the numbers. You will get the sum total of the number. Add the numbers in it. You will arrive at a number which would be your lucky number

# PREFACE

## Discover the Inner in You
## through Numerology

**N**umerology can assist and help you to understand your own deep inner nature, your life goals, your talents, your hidden characteristics, and the opportunities and challenges that you would be getting and facing in your life.

Now know your true personality through various forms of numerology and discover your destiny through the cosmic power of numbers with Numerology Profile known as personality reading.

1. Your lucky number is considered the most lucky and important number in a numerology.

2. It reveals the path that you'll be following through your life, and it's the prime number that indicates your hidden talents and the inherited abilities which helps you to go along your way of life.

This lucky number is derived by calculating the sum of the total of month, day and year of birth, and then reducing the sum to a single digit or main single number.

3. Here comes the Destiny Number

The second most important number in the queue of powerful number is Destiny Number.

It translates your natural abilities as well as your potential talents, related to your character trends. Many of us, inherit these talents and skills at birth, and further grows and matures as the individual gets into maturity.

Further to say that these talents and abilities and skill are of primary importance in a man's work and career too.

This destiny Number is arrived by calculating the sum values of the number adding all the letters in the name—for example, the letters with destined numbers which are in full name which appears on the certificate of birth.

4. Finally comes the main number termed as "SOUL NUMBER"

The Soul Number is again an important number in line of important numbers.

It indicates and shows your inner ability, your motivation as to what you want to be, want you, desire to do and the ability to fore see the obstacles that are occupied with this motivation.

This Soul number is of utmost importance influencing in determination of one's point of view and the principles on which the person acts.

Although the lucky number and the destiny Numbers are easy to visualize in a person, the soul number is a very personal and private number unless it is revealed through the proper use age of numerology.

5.  This Soul Number is derived by calculating the sum of the number values of all the vowels in the full name of the native with reference to its numerical value.

The Birth date describes several important personality characteristics, but it's the least important of the core numbers. It is the reduced form of the number of the day on which a native is born.

I would definitely like to express my sincere thanks to Ms. Alpa Shah Director, Travel Company of UK, encouraging me to pen down this book in the interest of the beginners of Numerology.

I am also grateful and thankful to A Partridge India A PENGUIN RANDOM HOUSE COMPANY for publishing my book.


DATED                                              Sd/—
MAY 9TH 2014                              BALDEV BHATIA

# INDEX

About Numerology ....................................................... 9

Introduction ............................................................... 15

Preface .................................................................... 19

Birth No 1 ................................................................. 25

Birth No 2 ................................................................. 28

Birth No 3 ................................................................. 32

Birth No 4 ................................................................. 35

Birth No 5 ................................................................. 38

Birth No 6 ................................................................. 40

Birth No 7 ................................................................. 43

Birth No 8 ................................................................. 46

Birth No 9 ................................................................. 49

Birth No 10 ............................................................... 52

Birth No 11 ............................................................... 54

Birth No 12 ............................................................... 57

Birth No 13 ............................................................... 60

Birth No 14 ............................................................... 63

Birth No 15 ............................................................... 67

Birth No 16 ............................................................... 70

Birth No 17 ............................................................... 73

Birth No 18 ............................................................... 77

Birth No 19 ............................................................... 80

Birth No 20 ............................................................... 84

Birth No 21 ............................................................... 87

Birth No 22 ............................................................... 90

Birth No 23 ............................................................... 94

Birth No 24.................................................................... 98

Birth No 25.................................................................... 102

Birth No 26.................................................................... 106

Birth No 27.................................................................... 109

Birth No 28.................................................................... 113

Birth No 29.................................................................... 116

Birth No 30.................................................................... 120

Birth No 31.................................................................... 123

# NUMEROLOGY AND PLANETS

Compound Numbers ............................................... 128

Compatibility with numbers.................................... 137

Number Ruled by Planet SUN................................. 142

Number Ruled by Planet MOON ............................. 143

Number Ruled by Planet JUPITER ......................... 145

Number Ruled by Planet RAHU .............................. 147

Number Ruled by Planet MERCURY ...................... 150

Number Ruled by Planet VENUS............................. 152

Number Ruled by Planet KETU NEPTUNE.............. 154

Number Ruled by Planet SATURN.......................... 156

Number Ruled by Planet MARS.............................. 158

Gems and Stone for numbers ............................... 161

Planets, Numbers and Alphabets ......................... 164

# CHAPTER 1

## Your Birth No 1 Numerology

Know About Your Self
Through Numbers

**W**e would now describe the birth number in detail and depth so as to make the readers understand the true value and meaning of it in depth.

READ WHAT YOUR BIRTH NO HAS TO SAY ABOUT YOU

IF YOU BORN ON THE 1, 10, and 19 OF ANY
MONTH YOUR BIRTH NO IS 1
ADD YOUR BIRTH DATE NUMBER

AND GET THE SINGLE DIGIT

FOR EXAMPLE 10=1+0=1, 19=1+9,=10=1+0=1,
28=2+8+=10=1+0=1

READ WHAT YOUR BIRTH NO.1 HAS TO SAY ABOUT YOU

In general ones are leaders, independent active, speedy, adventures, original and easily bored. One take a heroic stance in life and thrive on obstacles which they prefer to see as challenge

They are depressed when they are not achieving their ideals which are very strong and positive rarely unrealistic.

Ones love what is new in the fashion scene. They pride themselves on being up to that and ahead in their thinking. They identify with ground breakers pioneers achievers. They are dominant peoples with a great deal of fairs they are ambitious decisive and often have an ironic scene of humor.

You strive to stand in the first from the crowd. A natural leader you have a strong will and need to goal to work towards. You may run yours own business. You do not take no for an answer but have to push yourself to follow through (you tend to procrastinate). You like to plan rather than implement and are talented in diagnosis and troubleshooting.

You are the one of the most idealistic people but consider yourself pragmatic rather than emotional.

You may not be demonstrative emotionally but you love very deeply and are sometime romantic. You value loyalty very highly. You want things to be done correctly.

Special Quality of Number 1 natives

Number one (1) are the leaders. They have a strong drive and great ambition for getting success. They are independent and would not like to have restrictions on them in having to work with others.

They easily become frustrated with the routine works. Another quality being they are pioneers, initiators, and gamblers. Being creative; they possess a very rapid and keen mind. Always on the run and strive hard to become the leaders.

They also have excellent business instincts, can command and run big organizations and large business houses. They possess the neck of using information for a specific and useful purpose. Gathering of Knowledge becomes a special tool in their hands

Apart from the above they en power a broad vision and possess a great capacity of motivating others.

They generally inherit great will power, which get tested in their midyears of life having enormous energy and opportunity for accomplishment in their lives. The will power, inventiveness and determination are the keys factors to their success which brings them much good rewards, financial success and prosperity.

On the reverse side they are often open to the ideas of others, but are extremely stubborn rigid and hardheaded once they are attached and become possessive to their plans and schemes. It is in their interest that they must avoid laziness and rigidness, since they and more prone to anger and frustration, and have a tendency to force the issues in their favor, at times when things are not progressing and developing as quickly as they wished to.

# CHAPTER 2

## YOUR BIRTH NO 2
## Numerology

Know About Your Self
Through Numbers

READ WHAT YOUR BIRTH NO HAS TO SAY ABOUT YOU

IF YOU BORN ON THE 2,11,20,29

$11=1+1=2$, $20=2+0=2$, $29=2+9=11=1+1=2$

Hence your birth number comes to a total of 2

THE NUMBER TWOS

In general Twos are very sensitive emotional people. They do not have the one raging ambition but are content to work more in the back ground often as support for more dominant people. Two's analyze a situation and are conscious of the dynamics of emotional interrelationships at work and at home.

They tend toward perfectionism (even-net picking) and should be allowed to work at their own pace. They will do anything to bring harmony into situation and often they will stay with an unpleasant situation longer then they should. Two's tend to be plagued by worries that stem from a fear of the unknown.

Your social life and the mate are very important to your sense of wellbeing. You may find more accomplishment through having good friends then you do from your employment. You are easily affected from environment and should only work with people with whom you are compatible. In a conflict, you tend to be a peacemaker.

You may not let on what your real feelings are in the conflict. You may work long hours to please someone. You crave affection and usually remember other people's birthday. You reply conversation looking for things you might say or wondering if someone has an ulterior motive. You are high strung and should not overtax your talents for music and arts.

You love beautiful things but often don't want to push yourself to get them. You are patient and excel at detail work. Do not compare yourself and your accomplishment with those who may have more assertive or competitive numbers.

As the most feminine among all numbers, Number 2 is the most under estimated number when it comes to judging its power and strength. Hence it is mostly termed as the great feminine number.

As this number seeks to be quite understanding, tactful, diplomatic, and gentle and itself aloof, maintains itself by keeping silent, peaceful and will try to avoid confrontations as possible as possible as anything.

If we look at its shape, we would find and recognize a symbolic gesture of its survivor and an extremely mild force. Its shape and size is like a bent on its knees with its head and back bowed in humility and forgiveness, which makes it easy to recognize it as weak and powerless creature.

This is in sharp contrast to the powerful and the mighty and number 1, who does not allow itself to bow to anyone at any cost.

On the other hand, when the humble and feminine 2 finds itself under attack and burdened with a crushing weight, it allows itself to bend and bends as much as demanded.

If and when the weight is removed, its flexibility and its elastic, force come right back up to its normal position, just with no or little harm done and this number will continue to play its role.

The common strength and power of number 2 is resilient and lasting, just like its shape which largely beautifies its nature and beauty. There is much more to its eye, and it is often the true power behind its skill and caliber.

As we are familiar to the leadership and decisive qualities of birth no 1, which contradicts the advice of his greatest folly, the number 2 as number twos are smart and possess the underlying qualities and gives the direction to the people as what is to be done. This birth number people generally controls the path of certain events without anyone else knowing or acknowledging it .

Resulting the credibility going to the other birth number people whereas this birth number simply looks on to itself.

The best of number 2 natives is that when the credibility is taken by others they are not bothered at all and being the most patience number as these natives know that their time will come.

The other positive quality being is that even if they does not get the recognition they deserve, they often tend to take a special place in the hearts and minds of others due to their grace, style and their excellent taste in the field of music art and literature.

The 2 natives have the in-born quality and sense of music with proper rhythm which makes them popular among social people, and it is in their area of play and art that thy shines as a dancers good speakers and bold conversationalist. With the quality of social environment within them, which is perhaps their most important asset It is their sense of humor that is witty and self-depreciating.

# CHAPTER 3

## Your Birth Number Three Numerology

Know About Your Self
Through Numbers

IF YOU BORN ON THE 3, 12, 21,30

12=1+2=3, 21=2+1=3, 30=3+0=3=3

Hence your birth number comes to a total of 3

WHAT YOUR BIRTH NO 3 HAS TO SAY ABOUT YOU

BIRTH NUMBER THREE

Happy outgoing, forever, optimistic, vivacious, talkative, scattered all these describe the threes. Lovers of social life and recreation, Threes do not enjoy hard physical employment. They may excel at sales and will always have several projects going on at once. Work must feel creative for them to be happy. They are not overly concern about money or the future.

They are spontaneous and impulsive. They must learn to be focused and not overly self-indulge. When positive they bring joy and light to all situations. All Threes easily overcome physical illness.

They are charming quick to see the humor in any situation but can be somewhat unreliable. They may spread themselves over several projects because they like to keep themselves busy.

They are energetic, but easily distracted. Their social life is of a great concern to them. Having many friends they need to budget a sizeable amount of gifts because they are also generous.

They love spontaneous get-together and may be the one in the office to suggest the going out of drinks or taking up a collection for a birthday party.

They naturally embellish stories and events. You are known for youthfulness, certain intensity in style and while friends may laugh about your scattered ness, you are love by them.

As we are aware that numbers have their own unique qualities and personalities and each of them having different signs. To know a good understanding of how numbers influence and affect us, we ought to get to gather and know each single-digit number in detail as how a person carries his own, personality his weakness and his strength of will power.

Detail description of the unique combination and union between the numbers 1 and 2 has been penned above as the main numbers of the main number family while describing the deep contradiction in nature of each of the number and their personalities.

Now, we move on to what could be considered the result of their union:

The number 3, an extraordinarily talented child. They are like a small gifted kids who are still under the protection of its elders somewhat spoiled, and always in need of guidance. However, the most of the number 3 are in the field of creation.

The powerful feelings, ideas and visions of the imagination, person with number 3s will seek a career in art. Their social skills are also excellent.

Many are drawn to three in their charts and are even willing to forgive traits like a lack of focus and direction, a habit of coping others. Also a caliber to to finish projects and an not willing to take responsibility.

It is easy for number three to enjoy day-to-day life as long as everything is well, but when challenges arise it becomes quite evident, that most of the three's focus has been on that exterior, leaving its fortitude at bay. Number three succumbs to difficulties unless friends and family move in to support it.

Having birth date as 3 is likely to add a good of vitality to your life. The energy of 3 allows you to bounce back rapidly from all kinds of setbacks, be it mental or physical.

They have a natural ability to express themselves in public, and always make a very good impression. Good with words, they excel in writing, speaking, and possibly singing. They are energetic and always a good conversationalist. They are affectionate and loving, but sometimes too sensitive.

# CHAPTER 4

## Your Birth Number Four Numerology

Know About Your Self
Through Numerology

READ WHAT YOUR BIRTH NO HAS TO SAY ABOUT YOU
4 FOUR
IF YOU BORN ON THE 4. (FOURTH) OF ANY
MONTH THAN KINDLY READ THE FOLLOWING:

THE NUMBER FOURS

In general those with a birth date of Four are called the "salt of the earth". Loyal, productive, earnest, Fours love home, family, and country. They prefer secure environments and stability. They take a cautious approach and enjoy working with their hands.

They are builders and managers. While Fours are traditionalist they are also enthusiastic supporters of measure that result in reform, improvement and efficiency.

You succeed through business, management, production, and anything connected to building and the earth. You learn things the hard way and have confidence that you can learn anything if shown the principles.

You may have trouble seeing the "big picture". You can be very cautious and careful in approach to work and life in general. You must make an effort to keep up to date. With fundamentals no frill thinking you have strong ideas about the right way to do things. You may work on several manual jobs in your life before working your way up to a position where your experience is respected.

You make you a better manager and organizer. You may be more responsible and self-disciplined. Sincere and honest, you are a serious and hardworking individual. Your feelings are likely to seem somewhat repressed at times. You have on your ability to show and express affections, as feeling are very closely regulated and controlled.

For number four natives there is a good deal of rigidity and stubbornness associated with them as they happen to be Powerful, builder, egocentric, and unpredictable.

Non-conforming, strong, hard to keep up with energetically. Very mental, hard to grasp, like relating through a smokescreen, evasive. Good sense of order, keen observation skills. You radiate reliability and consistency. People trust you and feel secure with your judgment.

You are seen as a cornerstone of a business, and are relied upon to do you work efficiently and expertly.

You have strength and respectability. You tend to dress in a utilitarian manner, concerned mostly with convention, practicality, durability, Reliability Consistency and price.

You present yourself as someone who values correctness, control, and precision. You want to be judged on the basis of your performance, rather Minor Personality

You are frugal and have learned to respect the dollar. You are concerned about the security of your future and those you love; however, this may appear to others as a bit too austere.

# CHAPTER 5

## Your Birth Number Five Numerology

Know About Your Self
Through Numerology

READ WHAT YOUR BIRTH NO HAS TO SAY ABOUT YOU

5 FIVE
IF YOU BORN ON THE 5
(FIFTH ANY MONTH THAN KINDLY READ THE FOLLOWING:

THE NUMBER FIVES

In general, Fives are active, adaptable, curious people who insist on your independence. They prefer flexible hours and will always add a new dimension to whatever they do. Fives are very good sales people gregarious and persuasive. Fives love a good deal and want to be successful. They are spontaneous and know how to take advantage of an opportunity.

They move quickly and do not brood over losses. They are charming not always too serious and love being the devil's advocate. Fives open new territory, promote big business deals, and do not except the word "can't". A wariness in your nature may make you a bit impatient and easily bored with routine. You may have a tendency to shirk responsibility.

You enjoy traveling. You may want to marry late so that you call explore first. Adventures, you need work that is challenging, risky, and different. You would be a excellent promoter being something of a ham yourself.

You are known as a good storyteller and jokester and will learn much through love affairs. You tend to use things up quickly and seek new stimulation. You are inclined to work well with people and enjoy them. You are talented and versatile, very good at presenting ideas.

You are always on the alert, curious, and questioning and love to rock the boat. You will have a variety of jobs and will leave home early to seek your fortune, which, you are convinced in just around the corner. You see yourself as something of a hobo prince or lucky lady.

You may have a tendency to get itchy feet at times and need change and travel. You tend to be very progressive, imaginative and adaptable. Your mind is quick, clever and analytical.

# CHAPTER 6

## Your Birth Number six
## Numerology

Know About Your Self
Through Numerology

READ WHAT YOUR BIRTH NO HAS TO SAY ABOUT YOU

6 SIX
IF YOU BORN ON THE 6
(SIXTH THAN KINDLY READ THE FOLLOWING:

THE NUMBER SIXES

In general, those with a Six birth dates are the responsible type who prefer traditional lifestyle and domestic comfort. They are parents, teachers, practical artist, and healers.

They accomplish through their hands and hearts. Sixes are often plagued by worries, and will wither if not doing something useful.

Great community workers and upholders of moral justice, they understand compromise, and always search for an answer that serves the broadest interest. They are stubborn in their opinion as to what is "right".

You have a very loving, but territorial nature. You are natural teacher and your ideas on how to parent are strong. You are family-oriented and have a talent for settling disputes between people to the satisfaction of both sides. Your home is of the uttermost importance to you; you take responsibilities very seriously. You love luxuries and crave romantic attention.

On the other hand you may have unnecessary worries about going penniless, something which rarely happens to you since you are able to find easily financial backing for your business ideas.

Your social position and contacts are important to you. You know the value of reciprocity. Family and friends always come first.

With six as your birthdate you add tone of helpfulness, responsibility, and understanding to your natural instincts. You have a considerable amount of artistic talent. You have a deep appreciation of beauty and art. You are highly responsible and will do without in order to fulfill a debt . You are more apt to be open and honest with everyone, and more caring about family and friends. This is a number associated with utmost care and responsibility.

You must come to truly understand the ancient and fundamental principle of opposites that seek harmony. Whether the realm is the emotions, caring for others, finances, work, or play, you must learn where you can be of service, exactly what you can do, and what are your limits.

You want to help others, and you focus is on relationships. whereas a healer you could make a profession of the healing arts, either as a health therapist or doctor or a massager.

When you are praised you come to know that you are appreciated. On being criticized, on the other hand, leaves a very bad impression on you. You take it deeply to heart. You will sacrifice your own comfort to support and help others. You are generous, kind, and understanding. At times you can be highly emotional and given to extremes in sympathy and can be as loving as ever.

# CHAPTER 7

## Your birth Number Seven

Know About Your Self
Through Numerology

READ WHAT YOUR BIRTH NO HAS TO SAY ABOUT YOU

7 SEVEN
IF YOU BORN ON THE 7 (SEVENTH)
THE NUMBER SEVENS

In general, those with a seven birth date are unusual people with special talents. Intellectual and absorbed, they are often considered loner and lover of solitude. They generally love nature, animals, and serene environments.

Material success means less to them then being able to live life by their own rules. By nature they are deep peoples, intuitive and observant with spiritual and technical abilities. Seven are usually cautious and move very slowly when making decisions. Alcoholism is sometime a problem for sevens. They do not take advice well.

You will succeed if you will learn to concentrate on one thing at a time. Your intuition will lead you to the right opportunities and then you have to get specialized training in the field you have chosen.

You may have fine technical abilities. Your work may involve a great deal of research or you may be a farmer or a rancher, immersed in the land.

You tend to follow your hunches rather then someone else advise. You should realize that you have strong opinion that you may not want to compromise, and relationships may suffer from your intractability. You will find your opportunities coming to you though patient waiting; if you try to be aggressive, you may experience frustration at the pace of events. Never gamble. Your attitude of caution in regard to money is correct. You may play an esoteric instrument or have unusual hobbies and friends.

You have an affinity for the country and animals, and meditation and solitude are absolute necessities for you. You may be prone to be quite and have few special friends rather than many.

You like to spend time alone but have to be careful not to become too withdrawn. You need to meditate and do some spiritual exercise in order to develop your intuitive talents. You have par excellence intuition. Once you have begun to trust your intuition, you would have a sound faith.

You prefer to work alone and set your own pace. You tend to finish projects once started. Your interest leans to the scientific, technical, and metaphysical effects of life.

You are quite sensitive and feel deeply involved, in everything but you don't share your feelings that easily and tend not to communicate them to anyone. At times you can be stubborn. You can be highly critical and self-centered these trends can lead to unhappiness, if you are not careful.

You should specialize in one given field in order to make full use of your caliber and abilities and your natural intellectual talent.

# CHAPTER 8

## Numerology

Know About Your Self
Through Numerology

READ WHAT YOUR BIRTH NO HAS TO SAY ABOUT YOU

8 EIGHT
IF YOU BORN ON THE 8. (EIGHTH) ANY MONTH
THAN KINDLY READ THE FOLLOWING:

THE NUMBER EIGHTS

In general, Eight are hardworking, practical people. They are never without a desire to better their position and posses a knack for knowing how to do it. They have a natural self-confidence and do not stay in subordinate position for long. They are natural leaders and managers and, while they may be admire by their associates, are also somewhat feared.

They are not usually considered "one of the gang". As women Eight must acknowledge an ability to direct and achieve. Eight knows the power value and mechanic of money by second nature.

They may be strict, but are always fair and loyal to those who serve them. They may appear somewhat formal. They are dependable, objective, and dominant.

You are very ambitious person, highly motivated to do well. You will stop at nothing to move forward to your chosen work. You need a career of business that will challenge you.

You will not stay in a subordinate role, but will rise to the level of supervisor, manager, foreman, head of department, or professional very quickly usually through your own hard work unaided by "lucky breaks".

Women who were born on the 8th need to work outside the home. Eight will find the success in any large structured organization, such as factories, law firm, criminal justice system, military, financial institution, hospital or government. In business, you should be your own boss. You have a way with money and will do very well in life.

When success evades you, you have a tendency to become cynical or bitter. You are serious and mature, discipline and competent. You may have trouble sharing your emotional side with the opposite sex; as a woman you may seem very independent and dominant to men. Eight need a partner who is willing to differ them. You buy only name brands.

You must try to avoid partnerships wherever possible. You being highly competitive and when power is divided you indulge in intrigues and manipulation and snatch. You have the capability to handle large projects such as your departments and your own business.

On the negative side you have little patience with weakness. You do not express your feelings much.

Hence forth you are advised to develop the qualities of perseverance and tolerance. You will meet many obstacles, which must be viewed as challenges which will make you stronger. Your power of thinking and attitude towards the difficulties in life will be the difference between your failures and success.

# CHAPTER 9

## Numerology

Know About Your Self
Through Numerology

READ WHAT YOUR BIRTH NO HAS TO SAY ABOUT YOU

9 NINE
IF YOU BORN ON THE 9. (NINTH) OF ANY MONTH
THAN KINDLY READ THE FOLLOWING:

THE NUMBER NINES

In general, Nine are broad minded, idealistic, generous loving people with multiple talents. They are interested in universal good and often go into fields where there is broad scope. Music, Art, drama, healing arts, the ministry, metaphysics, social reform any area is open to them. They have a strong need to express the self, but not necessarily in the more ego-centered way of the One or Eight. Nines can be diffused and vague.

They are very vulnerable to outside influences and often experience difficulty in deciding what they are going to be or in making decision in general.

Young Nines may choose an eccentric life style to rebel against tradition.

They may or may not continue on that path depending on who they meet and the experiences that influence them. Nines need too learn not to take everything personally. They will take up causes and wonder why others are not so involved as they are. They will do well in groups that strives to reform and educate. All nines have dramatic style whether in their dress, speech, manner, or philosophy. They can be distant and cool.

You can succeed in any artistic, healing, teaching, philanthropic, or musical line of work. You are idealistic and emotional. Life is serious for you and you feel such a need to be of service to the world that you have trouble making up your mind about which carrier you follow. You are very capable but have some trouble concentrating on everyday details.

You become absorbed in whatever interest you and you have many interests. You may have a metaphysical outlook towards world problems. You will find yourself involved with much group work throughout your middle years. You may travel extensively and your life will always be full of surprises. You may be drawn to transformational work through therapy.

When you multiply any number by 9, then add the resulting digits and reduce them to a single digit, it always becomes a 9. For example, 5 x 9 = 45, reduce 45 to a single digit by adding them together: 4+ 5 = 9. Similarly, 7 x 9 = 63, and 6 + 3 = 9. Or 25 x 9 = 225, 2 + 2 + 5 = 9, and so forth.

When you multiply any number by 9, then add the resulting digits and reduce them to a single digit, it always becomes a 9. For example, 5 x 9 = 45, reduce 45 to a single digit by adding them together: 4+ 5 = 9. Similarly, 7 x 9 = 63, and 6 + 3 = 9. Or 25 x 9 = 225, 2 + 2 + 5 = 9, and so forth.

There is nothing similiar about this. Any number, no matter how large, multiplied by 9 reduces to 9. From a numerological perspective, the 9 simply takes over, like the infamous body snatchers. Any number that was initially increased by a factor of 9

The more you can be of service to humanity, the greater will be your personal reward on all levels You must have a keen sense of what will work, but at the same time directing those efforts toward some greater good. Your challenge is to find a place for yourself that has some direct benefit to others. Natives born on the 9th day usually take enough time before choosing a clear job or profession.

# CHAPTER 10

# Numerology

Know About Your Self
Through Numerology

READ WHAT YOUR BIRTH NO 10 HAS TO SAY ABOUT YOU

IF YOU BORN ON THE 10th

You have great deal of vitality and recover yourself from any setback. You are creative and have many interest and are always forward thinking. You may have little help from others because you structure situation so that you are I n dispensable You would do well in design.

You can become dull and even depressed if you are bound too tightly to the smaller details of life. You are often frustrated by routine activities. In order to rescue yourself from such a fate, it will be necessary to take prudent risks. You must learn to assert yourself. You are a pioneer at heart. You must live up to such a charge. You are highly competitive and can suffer from jealousy when it comes to the success of others.

On the positive side you have excellent managerial skills. You plan well and can organize people to carry out your plan. However you are often frustrated by similar and routine activities.

On the negative angle you can be stubborn and rigid when it comes to ideas that you feel strongly about. Yet, you are a loyal and devoted friend and can be demonstrative of your affections.

You are highly competitive and can suffer from jealousy when it comes to the success of others, especially colleagues or friends. By using the determination and creativity you possess, you can achieve much success.

Your positive qualities are leadership, forcefulness, optimism, strong convictions, competitiveness, creativity, progressiveness, independence, gregariousness.

Your negative traits are antagonism, lack of restraint, selfishness, weakness, overbearing, jealousy, egotism, pride, instability, impatience

# CHAPTER 11

## Numerology

Know About Your Self
Through Numerology

READ WHAT YOUR BIRTH NO 10 HAS TO SAY ABOUT YOU
IF YOU BORN ON THE 11th

11 ELEVEN
IF YOU BORN ON THE 11 (ELEVENTH) OF ANY MONTH
THAN KINDLY READ THE FOLLOWING:

THE NUMBER ELEVEN
IF YOU BORN ON THE 11th

Your birth date is the master of inspiration. All Twos are sensitive and this is especially true for you. This is the number of the teacher or of someone who function as exemplar. If you are female you may be unusually pretty. If male you may have refined characteristics or be interested in aesthetic pursuits. You may find yourself in the limelight. Successful areas are Television, poetry, metaphysics, art, psychology and spiritual work.

You have a tendency to fall in love with peoples and ideas. You may always be on the verge of success yearning to do something almost impossible. Eleven can fall into menial work while nurturing a strong sense that they are meant for better things. Try to find some talent that you can express.

Number 11 represents your connection to your subconscious, and to your instinct. as number 11 has all the qualities of 2, the negative points of the number follow with anxiety, shyness, stressed energy which is balanced out by the quality of number 2.

If you have 11 in your birth date you most likely will experience anxiety and fear. It's extremely powerful and capable of great things, when used correctly. You can create personal power and spiritual evolution. You should not deny your instincts, and your inner, guiding voice to push it to toward a great goal. Number 11 is a number of faith, and very much associated with psychics, saints and prophets.

Number 11 is a number with potentials which are difficult to live up to as you have the capacity to be irrational, and lead merely by your own living. However your inborn inner strength and awareness can make you an, social worker, philosopher, or advisor or an excellent teacher.

No matter what area of work you are into, you are quite aware and sensitive to the highest sense of your judgment and environment. Your intuition is strong; in fact, many psychic people and those involved in occult science have the number 11 as your own express. You possess a good mind with keen analytical ability. and you can probably succeed in most lines of work. You will do better outside of the business world. You are more content working with your ideals, rather than being practical in terms of money matters.

The positive aspects are idealistic attitude, long term thinking, far reaching effects of actions and plans, y our support and for art, music, and beauty in any form.

The negative qualities are associated with a continuous sense of nervous tension; you can at times be too sensitive and temperamental. You tend to dream a lot and may be more of a dreamer than a actioner, you are sometimes very impractical. You would like to spread the spat of your knowledge to others irrespective of their need and desire.

# CHAPTER 12

## Numerology

Know About Your Self
Through Numerology

READ WHAT YOUR BIRTH NO HAS TO SAY ABOUT YOU
12 TWELVE

IF YOU BORN ON THE 12 (TWELVE) OF ANY MONTH
THAN KINDLY READ THE FOLLOWING:

THE NUMBER TWELTH
IF YOU WERE BORN ON THE 12th

You have one of the most magnetic birth dates. You have an exceptional ability to express yourself, be convincing, and persuade others. Your mind goes right to the heart at any issue. You are idealistic, yet logical and can be brilliant.

You are easily bored and often tired of people ones you have picked their brains. You have a great need to charm and need to flirt. Your eye for color and design, especially in photography, is outstanding. You love the media-movies, magazines, television and keep up to date on who is whom. You are something of a celebrity of yourself. The number 12 is a complete cycle of experience and when an individual has number 12 as the birth number it leans towards a higher consciousness.

This number points to a group of developed souls who have accumulated an unusual inner strength. Their old habits need to be changed. The soul then attracts what it needs as a learning experience.

Number 12 should tend to be alert to every situation, to be suspicious of those who offer a false flattery and those who use it to gain their own ends.

Number 12 represents the learning process of all levels, and the sacrifice necessary to achieve the wisdom on both Spiritual and Intellectual levels. The number 12 generally need a partner who is honesty in their communication. They are quick to get attracted to people who are bright, happy, independent and lively.

Laughter is quite an important part of their lives and they have inquiring minds to collect data on interesting subjects because they enjoy mental stimulation and enjoyment of mental nature.

People get attracted towards them as they possess a wide range of knowledge about the world and its people. They don't like being told that they cannot do a thing . The more talented they become, about their abilities they become more cautious about it.

They possess a high degree of artistic talent that emerges in virtually everything. They take seriously, their home, cooking, the way they express themselves, when committed to.

They enjoy more entertaining people with stories, jokes, or witty remarks. They have plenty of vitality and are especially talented in the verbal and writing skills.

The positive aspects : imaginative and quick-witted versatile, energetic and professional, perceptive attributes and abilities family consciousness, friendly in their relationships, and rather shy.

# CHAPTER 13

## Numerology

Know About Your Self
Through Numerology

READ WHAT YOUR BIRTH NO HAS TO SAY ABOUT YOU

13 THIRTEEN

IF YOU BORN ON THE 13 (THIRTEEN) OF ANY MONTH
THAN KINDLY READ THE FOLLOWING:

THE NUMBER THIRTEEN
IF YOU WERE BORN ON THE 13th

You do well in business involved with manufacturing commerce real estate and building (especially remodeling). You are more capable of verbal expression then those born on the 4th and posses creative ability that absorb you. You would like to be more socially successful, find a great deal of satisfaction in your work. You have an exceptional ability to reform and improve any situation or condition. You may have strong emotional nature that erupts suddenly because you have tendency to ignore your feelings.

You have excellent concentration. Your discipline comes to rely upon you. You can work hard; need be careful not to become overworked to the point that you no longer take time to waste. Yet you may feel that you have to find the work that you truly would love to do or were meant for you. Your challenge is to make the most of what you are. There may be a feeling that your talents are buried. This can lead to try many different vocations and you may try to find some alternative against all odds. Your co-workers recognize your discipline and come to rely upon you. Your challenge is to make the most of what you are doing right now.

Using your considerable perseverance and determination. You need to raise the work you are currently responsible for to a high value of favorable result.

You would also need to cultivate faith and a willingness to apply yourself to the in order to develop such an attitude, or else you may wander from job to job, relationship to relationship friendship to friendship.

You can be stubborn and rigid, and this can, and lead to frustration and depression for you. Things seem to take to reciprocation, especially when you resist bringing fresh approaches into your unique ways of doing things.

The ways to your success are your willingness to discipline in your life, and make the most of every opportunity that comes your way in terms of being a winner and a successful person.

You have a great love for your family, its tradition and the community. You are the architect of any work you commit to, you get your work done with great zeal and accuracy.

You possess a considerable amount of talent and are always looking for some solid form of expression. Your subordinates get impressed with your discipline and come to trust on you. You may feel that you have yet to found the work you truly love to do.

You may also have a feeling that at times your talents are buried in depth and it becomes difficult or you to find them and your challenge would be to make the most of it to search and find them.

The nature is guiding you. You need to make a habit of faith and apply yourself to the matter when at work. If you refuse to develop such an habit, you may wander from job to job, relationship to relationship and friendship to friendship.

Your positive qualities: initiative ambition, creativity, independence, self-expression, love of freedom

Your negative nature: unemotional, rebelliousness impulsiveness, indecision, bossism, and at times cruelty.

# CHAPTER 14

## Numerology

Know About Your Self
Through Numerology

READ WHAT YOUR BIRTH NO HAS TO SAY ABOUT YOU

14 FOURTEENTH

IF YOU BORN ON THE 14 (FOURTEEN) OF ANY MONTH
THAN KINDLY READ THE FOLLOWING:

THE NUMBER FOURTEEN
IF YOU WERE BORN ON THE 14th

You may have most interesting life, studded with setbacks that cannot keep you down. You must be careful to know your boundaries. You will meet people throughout your life with whom you feel a "karmic" connection.

You are talented and versatile, competitive vigorous and can be discipline when there is some short term goal to be gained. You are, very good at presenting ideas, and you are also very good at organization and systematizing. You like to experiment and crave stimulation. You should be in business for yourself; anything to do with travel, Promotion, the public, performing and entertainment appeals you also you are inclined to work well with people and enjoy them. But often restlessness in your nature may make you a bit impatient and easily bored with routine, and rebel against it. You have a tendency to shirk responsibility.

You may have a tendency to get itchy feet at times and need change and travel. You tend to be very progressive, imaginative and adaptable. Your mind is quick, clever and analytical.. You want to live, not just exist. You may have a very opinionated nature based on what you have "experienced in the past". You have a highly visible sexual nature. You may be eccentric at times and may call for help.

You need to learn independence, self-initiative, unity and justice. Your great need in life is to achieve temperance, prudence, balance, harmony, and patience in life. You have the zeal power and motivation to make a success in anything you think to do. You are also warm and have a great deal of natural wisdom with new creative ideas.

You are also the one who possess everlasting movement and tend to bring trials and dangers from a great variety of experiences. You people at times experiment for the sake of experience only. Such behavior may lead you to chaos, but finally your aim is to try for progressive change and the final joy of growth and renewal.

People with number fourteen as your number are warm-hearted and naturally creative. They are quick to learn independence, self-initiation, unity and justice. They are very single minded need a constant challenge, however, or they may quickly become bored.

This is a number of attractive characteristics and they tend to attract the opposite sex. They are polite and diplomatic and have a lot of good friends. They can only think and work with one thing at a time. They are known to possess a great deal of wisdom, which they freely share with others. If they act cautiously they can be fortunate in money matters or business transactions. If anyone gives them too many things to think of at any one time they become decidedly vague.

People of number 14 are both make progress in the material field, but when it is loneness; they are put off by friends. From it they need to get rid of. Their mindsets are negative, and this complicates the relationship. They must have their mind set on a bed of more positive and power the strength of their good qualities.

They have the tendency to be born with money greed. They succeed in substantive matters, they carry with them the leadership skills, initiative, energy, mind, that they can bring to the acquisition of money.

For the following people their spouses and friends must be very rich, otherwise they cannot hope for good relations. These people are not very sincere, and they are hard to love.

On the other hand spouses of these people need to have the same materialistic. They are unable to cope with people who have a different mindset. They do not need those who do not care about money. On sexual event they are strong people, but also in the field of their. Number 14 people are opportunists and use people according to their needs and when they are no longer needed, do not seem care for them, thus gaining lot of enemies. Being somewhat pessimistic, it is suspicious. Such people are extremists and they are falling from one extreme to another.

These people are very active and steady in their work and they have the faith to succeed in it. They will not get entangled in unnecessary update complications like the other number natives.

Like a child, they freely mix with others. They pretend to speak from the bottom of their heart without hiding anything.

Their positive qualities: Their minds travel fast like electric current. They have the ambition to accomplish what is impossible for others to achieve. They are experts in attracting others towards them. They have excellent taste in jewelry, luxury articles and perfumes

Their negative nature: strong negative influences on other people and keep their negativities in check. They must concentrate only on ways of improving and elevating themselves. Nobody can fully understand them. Where it is necessary, they will talk in an engaging manner. Where' silence is more effective, they keep quiet and achieve their object.

# CHAPTER 15

## Numerology

Know About Your Self
Through Numerology

READ WHAT YOUR BIRTH NO HAS TO SAY ABOUT YOU

15 FIFTEEN

IF YOU BORN ON THE 15 (FIFTEEN) OF ANY MONTH
THAN KINDLY READ THE FOLLOWING:

IF YOU WERE BORN ON THE 15th

Your home is very important to you. You have great financial protection (all Sixes do), and people come to you for advice. You are more open-minded, spirited, independent, and well traveled then other Sixes.

If female, you need a carrier outside the home (although you consider your home an accomplishment in itself ). You would make great fashion or interior designer, emergency nurse, or teacher.

You need a wide social circle of educated people as friends. Your family is your first priority, but friends soon become "family" to you. You can be quite creative. Singing is a possible talent; at the very least, you will be noted for a pleasing voice.

You tend to be attracted to unusual people or situations. You also enjoy the security of a settled family life and the need to feel the frequent expression of their partner's love. The more aloof you seem, the more you are in need of affection. Your emotions are powerful, and you can usually use them to your advantage rather than letting them overwhelm you. This creates quite a complex, but gentle and loving vibration.

You are an independent person who can be quite rebellious at times. You can give an impression that you are an extremely tough guy but in reality you are very sensitive, vulnerable and soft, and loving people. You also don't allow others to get too close until they trust you, but it is worth the effort because you are very loyal, and faithful.

Your relationships may be a little challenging. You work largely on your thoughts and instincts, although you are sometimes quite stubborn, you are quite versatile and somewhat restless. Your mind is so sharp and your talents many, that you may change your career path more than a few times in your life.

Your emotions are powerful, and you can usually use them to your advantage rather than letting them overwhelm you. Although you may enjoy an increase in your intuitive capabilities, you may also be too open to influence that fears or delusions impact your ability to see your life clearly. You are very responsible and capable. You like harmony in your environment and strive to maintain it. You tend to learn by observation rather than study and research. This number shows artistic leanings. You being a generous and giving person, a bit stubborn in ways, you may experience passive-aggressiveness in others, which impacts your life in frustrating ways

Your mind is fertile, and you are able to blend practical thinking with imagination. You can talk your way into, or out of, almost anything. You can be successful in an artistic area. Your great imagination and ability to understand and formulate artistic ideas are big assets.

You are very likely to attract loving relationships and/or new warm social contacts into your life. Your popularity increases and efforts to smooth over challenges in partnerships are more likely to succeed.

At times, however, you could struggle with variable energy and motivation levels. Be aware of a tendency to be attracted to impractical ventures. You may find that is too easy to waste your time and energy, perhaps due to a lack of drive or feeling directionless. They are very kind and having more patience. They never give heed to small diseases. How much pain or suffering they may be getting, but they do not express their diseases properly. These are the people with full of happiness and happy going.

If the planetary position is not favorable in their chart specially the planet Venus than they react in a negative way and bring dangers to their karakas. Rather than becoming lover they may become greedy, wrong minded and can have bad habit like drinking seen and these things make them more dangerous.

Their positive qualities: fertile mind, loving relationships, practical thinking, harmony in environment, learn by observation and and ability to understand. Affectionate, simple, luxury liking, lover, liking poetry, music etc

Their negative nature: struggling with variable energy and motivation levels, sometimes quite stubborn, somewhat restless at times and in need of affection.

# CHAPTER 16

## Numerology

Know About Your Self
Through Numerology

READ WHAT YOUR BIRTH NO HAS TO SAY ABOUT YOU

16 SIXTEEN

IF YOU BORN ON THE 16 (SIXTEEN) OF ANY MONTH
THAN KINDLY READ THE FOLLOWING:

IF YOU WERE BORN ON THE 16th

Yours is one of the most unusual birthday number. It bring startling events which become turning point in your life. Your friends will be highly unusual. You may chosen an eccentric lifestyle and always have a feeling that you are somehow different. The 16 is a karmic number.

This may mean that you have connections with people based on past life experiences and you will feel a special quality when you meet them-or by the way you meet them. Life is never dull with the 16. Many things are learned the hard way. You do not take undue risks.

Your attitude may complicate your working or marital situations. Because of the nature slowness of the Sevens, you may procrastinate. You are analytic and may pursue technical or historical fields. You may uncover facts of great significance or invent something entirely new. You insist that friends be of high quality. You may love antiques and stamp collections.

You consider love as the most beautiful thing and you love to fall in love, but a number of your group members think that the person they love is not sincere with them. You love to be with your friends and you are always found to be a dutiful friend. You can hardly control your patience, which is a very big drawback of your nature. gives a sense of loneliness and generally the desire to work alone. You are relatively inflexible, and insist on your being independent. You need a good deal of time to rest and to meditate. You are introspective and a little stubborn. Because of this, it may not be easy for you to maintain permanent relationships, but you probably will as you are very much into home and family. They have got the strong tendencies of exploring the hidden meaning behind situations and circumstances. You are considered to be very knowledgeable and your intellectual level is very high.

You are known for taking wise decisions and are very good in researches. The only problem with you are with is that you keep most of the knowledge to yourself. That's where you need to get improved. The knowledge and learning gets better when you share it with others. Let you be known for your intellectual achievements and ideas rather than to keep them as a secret.

Share your perspective with others. This will make this earth planet a better place to live in. Secrecy beyond a level doesn't help you in achieving anything in life. Nor does you allow success in your love. Even though you try hard you find it difficult to hold on to your lover. The love melts and slips through your life.

You are more interested in the occult. You gain knowledge in, numerology, astrology and occult sciences. You research into religion and spirituality. You believe in simple living and high thinking.

This unique number 16 says that even if you make money you do not enjoy your riches. You think that others around you lead a false life. You want to guide them to your path of purity and simplicity.

Your birth number sixteen inclines to interests in the technical, the scientific, and to the religious explorations. You may be emotional, but have a hard time expressing these emotions. Because of this, there may be some difficulty in giving or receiving affection.

Your positive qualities: Charming, lively, Intuitive, spiritual, possess self-control, perfectionist, reliable friends, Proud, investigative, philosophical, rational thinking and positive thinking.

Your negative traits: unpredictable, surrender to emotions, prone to withdrawal when emotionally troubled, Trouble expressing feelings, stubborn, cynical unsure, escapist, to partner-with.

# CHAPTER 17

## Numerology

Know About Your Self
Through Numerology

READ WHAT YOUR BIRTH NO HAS TO SAY ABOUT YOU

17 SEVENTEEN

IF YOU BORN ON THE 17 (SEVENTEEN) OF ANY MONTH
THAN KINDLY READ THE FOLLOWING:

IF YOU WERE BORN ON THE 17th

You are dynamic go-getter. You have the daring and courage to undertake large projects and the executive ability to delegate to the right people. You have one of the best business and financial outlook possible.

Your business may be at the cutting edge of its industry. You have vision and determination-unbeatable qualities. If you are male, opposite sex will be highly attracted to your power. If female, you will instill admiration in others, although you ay need to emphasize your feminine qualities to attract men.

The number should attain the highest achievement; integrity is the key. Your judgment is nearly infallible and you are outstanding troubleshooter. Do not get bogged down with details delegate! You admire scholars and historians and will excel in technical, factual writing. You are never vague, you are very fortune financially, as seventeen is very good for business interest. Although you are probably very honest and ethical, this number at times forces you to be shrewd but however hard it be you would successful in the world of business and commercial enterprise. You have excellent organizational, managerial, and administrative skills and knowledge along with capabilities enabling you to handle large projects with ease.

You are ambitious and highly goal-oriented and you have very sound judgment. You are an excellent manager and organizer. You are gifted with the ability to see the larger picture. Sensitiveness in your nature, often repressed you to fall below the surface of awareness, makes it hard for you to give or receive affection. You are blessed with excellent business and financial instincts. Your approach to business is original, creative and daring. You are highly independent. Whether it is business or socially oriented, your ambitions spread out far and wide and you will not rest until you have placed your mark on the world. Your challenge is to avoid becoming obsessed with your own judgment and power to the point that you refuse to delegate authority or responsibility to others.

You are able to take life as it is, and they take the material values of life as something, which is supposed to be here, because of the inner tranquility. You have a strong character, and life circumstances cannot break your spirit. You are self-confident and have high expectations of yourself. The expectations of others stimulate you, especially if they doubt you can pull off what you intend to do. You tend to be egoistic and dramatic, especially with money. You have a need for status and may show off the fruits of your labor with impressive items. You and only you have sufficiently sound judgment to guide the ship and tend to sail the same in your own way. You need to avoid being possessive of your enterprise. You ought to Share the fruits of your labors with others, which will multiply your pleasure manifold if tried. Laurels for you, always set new goals.

People with seventeen as their number always believe in their good luck and their own strength They usually think well before they do something.

They have the ability to see perspective and, most importantly, see how different things appear to them in the perfective. Those born under Number 17 are able to work effectively and implement large projects. They also like to receive a significant social status. Some of them may be too much addicted to money and properties.

People born under Number 17 are very volatile and restless by nature. Therefore they often rootless cannot keep the balance and it is difficult for them to be seriously attached to one and same person for a long time in the early period of their lives.

They have to start and end several relationships to find the right spouse. Such people are always Looking ahead for unwanted changes in relationship. Due to their constant changes these people are very confused because they never know what they will do next. They like to change partners from time to time, but such deviations do not affect the ongoing relationship. At times they are strangely dependent on the feelings of others, though they are quite capable of doing things on their own. They need to bear in mind that the solution to any problem does not depend on other people, but it comes itself within them only to achieve success.

Your positive qualities:

Strong constitution, action motivated, goal oriented, good judgment of character, slow, business minded, materially focused. wealth, fame and fortune .Prefer to work alone and accomplish much.

Your negative traits: Argumentative, manipulative, problems with authorities, stubborn, frustrated by limitations. Generally struggles with opposition, delays, failures, humiliation. Get entangled with the law and substance abuse, prone to addictions and depression and extreme states of consciousness. Suicidal tendencies, easily feel unwanted, unloved, neglected and rejected.

# CHAPTER 18

## Numerology

Know About Your Self
Through Numerology

READ WHAT YOUR BIRTH NO HAS TO SAY ABOUT YOU

18 EIGHTEEN

IF YOU BORN ON THE 18 (EIGHTEEN) OF ANY MONTH
THAN KINDLY READ THE FOLLOWING:

IF YOU WERE BORN ON THE18th

You can accomplish very great things when you put your mind to it. You have the drive and ambition of the one and the executive capacity of the Eight. You will have to push yourself a bit to get through the obstacles that will force you to acquire more knowledge and understanding.

As a child you may have displayed a nature kind of maturity. You will not like to take advice from others. Your own critical power are good and could be used professionally (especially in drama, art. And music). You definitely need to work the good for others.

You have a great sense of dignity, and you like when other people appreciate them. Some of you seek to be either too flexible or too stubborn. When something goes wrong you may experience fear, anxiety, and uncertainty. You understand others and are quite aware of the developed situation, as you are always able to find a common language with different people.

You dream of traveling to another countries, are interested in other people's lives. Sometimes you may go too far in your dreams and dive into the world of illusions. You seek some diversification in lives, experimenting in different areas. You need to balance the romantic attitude to life and it must be done through common sense.

Number 18 natives need to learn to accept the world and people as they are. Also they should get rid of all negative attachments which at times get aggregated. The spiritual and philosophical approach to all cases, care for the others will help Number 18 to avoid illusions and live a real and charming life.

Number 18 are mainly controlled by the Number nine . These people are very sexy, but it is not so easy for them to express their desires and dreams. To express their desire seems to them shameful, they often take it as a sign of weakness. There is also the influence to prevail in the affairs of heart.

For Number eighteen, the partner should be soft and flexible and should play a leading role in sex, because of which Number 18 cannot explicitly express feelings and desires. In friendship people of Number 18 are very faithful, although it is not easy to get along with them on the other side, the Number 18 is the dominant character and does not let people to impose their decisions on them.. Although natives of Number 18 are not so easy to get along with, but these people are very interesting companions, being smart and positive. People of Number 18 may become a perfect friends for those who have the same spiritual qualities and ambitions. People Born under

Number 18 may not understand someone who is lacking ambition, because for them it is the driving force, and people without ambitions they see as weak-siblings. So they cannot deal with them.

same energy, but can tolerate them, here is also shown the influence of Number 8. Despite their dominant nature, those born under Number 18 can be a very good friends, because Number 8 gives them enough sensitivity and inhibits their desire to command. Still for the sake of friendship people should not contradict much to Number 18.

People of Number 18 should study how to be softer, otherwise they are at risk to lose the friends that they have. They can be an excellent leaders—intelligent and hardworking, but when they start to treat others rudely, they become unpopular. Not everyone can understand them as their loved ones do. They should not be impatient with those who disagree with them. If they are able to overcome these negative traits and tendencies, they can become a very pleasant and wonderful people, and rise to even greater heights.

Your positive qualities: desire to command, driving force, express their desires and dreams, spiritual and philosophical approach, critical power good, have the drive and ambition, excellent leaders—intelligent and hardworking.

Your negative traits: very sexy, not like to take advice from others. to be impatient, not so easy to get along, too flexible and too stubborn, interested in other people's lives, often drives into the world of illusion.

# CHAPTER 19

## Numerology

Know About Your Self
Through Numerology

READ WHAT YOUR BIRTH NO HAS TO SAY ABOUT YOU

19 NINTEEN

IF YOU BORN ON THE 19 (NINTEEN) OF ANY MONTH
THAN KINDLY READ THE FOLLOWING:

IF YOU BORN ON THE 19th

Take note this is one of the four Karmic numbers and signifies that you have chosen some special direction or have a special goal in life you will always being trying to fulfill It; your nature is complex due to the combination of the one and the nine. Extremely discerning and perceptive you may put up an aloof or formal front use your intellect as a shield until you get to know someone.

Verbal sparring and a keen sense of humor usually a dry wit characterize your social interaction your emotional attachment are deep but you strive to maintain self-control at all times your negative attribute is often cynicism, rigidly, or xenophobia.

People born on 19th possess greater will power and self-confidence, and are often seen to be in original approach and a somewhat self-centered. Their ability and desire to handle details are amazing in approach. They are sensitive; they have a compelling manner that can be dominating in many situations. They do not tend to follow convention or take advice. Consequently, they tend to learn through experience; at times hard experiences. The number nineteens may be experiencing the feeling of being alone even if they are married. And there may be tendency to on the side of being nervousness and anger. These people always need more. They have a strong personality.

These people can destroy everything that stands in the way of their ambition. As a result they become corrupted by power. They believe and will never agree that a different kind of work could be done better. They are never content with what they have. They can force others to change their views about themselves in the desired direction of their personality. Also, there they want to be leaders.

In some respects these people are very sexually. They do recognize the obstacles when they want something from others. Special things can be said about their emotional life and sexual life.

They are great egotists and can simply reject the partners when it is no longer needed. Emotions in their lives do not matter much, even If they occur close to people, they will still be lonely. Number Nineteen natives are able to inspire full confidence in themselves, their magnetic personality takes over the possession of others. Spouses must be either the same or a completely obey them or become either equal, or slaves.

In sexual terms they cannot be satisfied, because they have always something missing. Since they cannot express their wishes, it become difficult for them to understand and the actions to be managed by a partner, but if the partner does not respond, these native go in for the use of force.

Natives with Number 19, as their number are very domineering, and those who are associated with them are likely live with fear, not because of affection. On the other hand, those who are faithful would be equally suit them well.

People who are born under this number will have the aspect of the sun with the result they will similarly remain solid and steadfast in their position. They will be mainly responsible for contributing to the welfare of their country. Therefore quite a few of them may be either politicians or top government officials. Some will work as great industrialists giving jobs to many people. They may adorn such positions as administrators, chairman, and financiers. If the sun's aspect is not in its full strength, their success will be less in proportion to the extent of the capacity and ability.

People born with this number would get success in their early years. They will be selected as class commanders, leaders or school leaders. Even if they have not have liking for leadership, others will force them to accept it.

The main reason behind their early success is from childhood onwards they lead an honest life and they have the capacity to perform their duties in best manner.

In short, people who have number 19 as their birth Number are born leaders. They can be looked up to; their personal judgment can be trusted; and they can inspire with warm the hearts of those around them.

As per numerology, name number 19 promises continuous growth. Your rank, position, status, and riches will keep on increasing.

Your positive qualities: continuous growth, positions as chairman, financier or administrator, full confidence, greater will power, magnetic personality,

Your negative traits: dominating in many situations, corrupted by power, cynicism, rigidly, or xenophobia, great egotists and very domineering.

# CHAPTER 20

## Numerology

Know About Your Self
Through Numerology

READ WHAT YOUR BIRTH NO HAS TO SAY ABOUT YOU

20 TWENTH

IF YOU BORN ON THE 20 (TWENTH) OF ANY MONTH
THAN KINDLY READ THE FOLLOWING:

IF YOU BORN ON THE 20th

You are extremely conscientious person, friendly, compassionate, and eager to help. You may do well in small business but will probably not want to take on a large project without help from others. Your high sensitivity makes you aware of other people's feelings. You also act considerately. You must develop the ability to truly see how necessary you are to the success of any enterprise you enter. You are the glue that binds projects together.

You will be attracted by spiritual matters and do quite a bit of searching through out your life. You would make a sensitive therapist, artist, photographer, or writer on subject of interest of women. You are apt to have a rather nervous air in the company of a large group.

You work slowly because of attention to detail. You need to order to help you from feeling anxious. You have an obstinate mind. Outwardly they pretend to be brave. You can make good progress in life if they develop faith in God. Your mind is always absorbed in imaginary world, research programs and drawing plants for the future. You have a warmhearted nature and emotional understanding that constantly seeks affection. You always be thinking either about their future or about a past incident. When you are alone, you get inspiration for new ideas. You are very prone to become depressed and moody, as emotions can turn inward and cause anxiety and mental turmoil and may not agree with the other. If you cultivate devotion and faith in god, they get themselves the power of self-confidence and can achieve things easily than anybody. You are a cooperative partner and hate to be alone.

Your talent lies in your keen insight and your willingness to act as an advisor to those who are able to wield power. You are especially moved by beauty, harmony and love. You give affection and need much in return. You are effective speakers, lawyers and salesmen of luxury items. You will help people to accomplish things. But when you have a personal problem to solve, you become frightened and you especially need physical affection, that is, plenty of hugs and warmth.

and the most striking quality about you is their power of imagination. You people possess imaginative and creative powers than anyone else. When you are filled with negative thoughts about your future you drag yourself to low self-esteem and you start to live your life mounted with fear and anxiety. You can become powerful if you know how to kill your low esteem with their self-confidence and devotion. In addition to that the twenty born people usually act slower but their thought process is very fast as their mind constantly thinks of something new to be tried.

Natives with 20th day of the month as your birth day add a degree of emotion, sensitivity, and intuition to your readings and approach towards your life. The facial energy provided here is very social, allowing you to make friends easily and quickly. Yet It can be hard for you to bounce back to reality when depression sets in. You are highly sensitive and very impressionable.

People with 20 as their number are prone to great awareness and can easily recognize the feelings of outsiders, even when they try to hide their inner thoughts. They are highly emotional as well, and are easily influenced by their own environment.

You are diplomatic modest, and polite. All of this creates a great need to develop and maintain your own caliber and thinking. Once you have accomplished any task, your life becomes more manageable and less threatening. You are less an more one who sees a project through to completion. You are good with details and can attract any one's attention.

Your positive qualities:
Diplomatic modest, and polite. Easily moved by beauty, harmony and love, high sensitivity, imaginative and creative powers, effective speakers, lawyers and salesmen.

Your negative traits: easily influenced by own surrounding and environment, highly emotional. act slowly, prone to become depressed and moody

# CHAPTER 21

## Numerology

Know About Your Self
Through Numerology

READ WHAT YOUR BIRTH NO HAS TO SAY ABOUT YOU

21 TWENTH FIRST

IF YOU BORN ON THE 21 (TWENTY ONE) OF ANY MONTH
THAN KINDLY READ THE FOLLOWING:

IF YOU WERE BORN ON THE 21st

**Y**ou may be a bit quieter and less impulsive then other Threes, very sensitive and more likely to think things through before speaking. You have a great imagination and may be prone to dreaming, perhaps writing poetry. You may be natural singer or songwriter. You may be content to have fewer, but closer friends then other Threes.

You are high strung and should avoid analyzing things too much. You may find you have a tendency of infatuations (due to seeing people in a rosier light through your imagination and sense of drama). You may be gullible. You love pleasure and aesthetic pursuits. You definitely avoid manual labor if at all possible.

You would have the energy to bounce back rapidly from early setbacks, of physical or mental nature. At times there would restlessness in your nature, but you seem to be able to show an easygoing attitude and nature in you, You have a special and natural ability to express yourself in public, and you always make a very good impression on others.

You dream of artistic expression; writing, painting, music. You would seek to more freely express your inner feeling and obtain more enjoyment from life. You also dream of being more popular, likable, and appreciated .Good in literary pursuits, you excel well in singing writing, and speaking, You are energetic and always are good conversation.

You have a good and keen imagining power, and are talented in writing and verbal skills. But it is often seen that you generally tend to waste your energies and become involved with too many things which are unnatural and superficial.

Your mind is quite practical emanation and rational despite having this tendency and you are able to jump out of the awkward situations. You are quite affectionate charming and loving, but at the same time very sensitive. You are subject to rapid ups and downs in your life and you often take it as a very serious matter.

You are highly creative, a vivacious soul and dynamic a creature who carries immense vigor & energy and believes in living every moment of life.

You are generally possessed with a strong will to succeed. You have a social gift. Your imagination is highly charged. You get along well with others and generally enjoy people's company and their environment condition. You are quick witted and can think on your feet. Both your mind and body are vital and seemingly sparklingly with life.

You are talented in verbal skills, scribbling, writing and speaking. You can be a successful, writer, editor cum artist. You are energetic inspiring and enthusiastic and willing to learn whatever comes in your way. You can uplift or enlighten a party or social gatherings and may serve as the life of the party. You feel pleasure in becoming a limelight of your social gatherings. You are an excellent speaker and salesman. Your focus your energies deeply in a specific field make the most of your life as winner.

Your imagination runs out of control. You must develop yourself and your talents in order to make the most of your life. You can easily let charm and wit pass for outstanding work. Your challenge is to ground and focus your energies deeply in a specific field or subject. Your love runs deep and you can be passionate. More often you seem to be on the receiving end of affection, simply because people are charmed by you or attracted to your charismatic and dynamic personality.

People with 21 as their number are the ones who would party hard after working hard as they are sincere personalities but never forget to live life. The people with this number carry a great charisma in their presence and are magnetic other people generally like to be with them.

Positive qualities : creative, a vivacious writer, editor cum artist. Charismatic and dynamic personality inspiration, creativity, love unions, long lasting relationships and verbal skills Negative traits: imagination runs out of control disappointment, fear of change dependency, nervousness, over emotionalism, lack of vision, and unnecessary involvement in too many things.

# CHAPTER 22

## Numerology

Know About Your Self
Through Numerology

READ WHAT YOUR BIRTH NO HAS TO SAY ABOUT YOU

22 TWENTH SECOND

IF YOU BORN ON THE 22 (TWENTY TWO) OF ANY MONTH
THAN KINDLY READ THE FOLLOWING:

IF YOU WERE BORN ON THE 22nd

This minister number requires you to work for the universal good rather than for personal ambition. This means that spiritual study should be a large part of your education. You are competent at almost anything you undertake.

You will find that your varied experience will some day be appropriate in a very challenging project. Your work must meet your ideals; you may pursue a hobby because you feel it will eventually pay off. You are not interested in status or luxury, but in making a significant contribution and living your life in a meaningful manner.

You will recognize a special quality in others. You are subject to a good deal of nervous tension. You can be single minded and realize your power is channeled from above. You are sensitive, analytical, and capable of handling large scale undertakings, with immense power to judge and having the capacity of assuming of working long and hard towards their completion.

Especially in your early years of your life, there is rigidity or stubbornness in you, and you tend to hide that feeling. Idealistically, you work for the greater cause with a good deal of inner strength and power within you. You have the qualities of an orderly and patient fellow. You can easily approach a problem methodically and systematically and can solve it without much difficulty. You are very aware and intuitive powers within you.

You possess the capacity to start your enterprise small and take practical steps toward enlarging it to its full scope. For greater strength, you can be deeply afraid of the dimensions of your ambitions. If your challenge is to be done willing you have a gift for seeing both the details of a plan and how it should be unfolded although you may secretly feel that nothing will measure up to your original dream.

You have a strange character. You like both good and bad. But the evil elements in bad attract you more. Therefore, you will look for special opportunities to drift into evil ways. With this subsequently, you can turn away from your goal and ambitions and this results in sad result with disappointment knocking at resulting in the sacrifice of your dream because of fear of failure.

Your solutions tend to be unique. You have good talents to make money. You keep your own counsel and have much inner strength. You will win in competitions, races, gambling, and other speculative games. On the other hand you can be nervous and suffer grave doubts about yourself, which you also tend to hide from others. Making it possibility that you will be surrounded by people who wait for exploiting your weakness.

Therefore, you need to be more careful even with your near and dear. You have to keep a constant watch over your friends too. Any one of them or a group of these persons can cheat you. You need to work for the universal good rather than for personal ambition. This means that the spiritual study in you should be, in greater part of your

career. You are competent at almost anything you undertake. You will find that your varied experience will someday be appropriate in a very challenging project. Your work must meet your ideals with which you may pursue a hobby because you feel it will eventually pay off.

You are not interested in status or luxury, but in making a significant contribution and living your life in a meaningful manner. You may have many friends. You will recognize a special quality in others. Your number as twenty-two will also display originality, competence and reformative abilities. You can be single minded and serious and need to feel in control. You must realize your power is channeled from above. You are sensitive, analytic, and judgmental.

Due to the intense vibration people with number twenty two as their birth no are born to get the sense of obligation in life and purity of consciousness. Quite often they tend to face amazing events have challenging years of early life, yet they often lead extraordinary lives after learning to utilize their full potential.

Positive qualities: master builder. Great accomplisher. unique qualities unorthodox approach to problem solving. strong leader, can in a positive vein, you possess practical approach, idealist, development inner strength is charisma to attract a the world.

Negative Traits: negative expression unorthodox methods, eccentricity. Dominating at times confused and over commanding.

# CHAPTER 23

## Numerology

Know About Your Self
Through Numerology

READ WHAT YOUR BIRTH NO HAS TO SAY ABOUT YOU

23 TWENTY THIRD

IF YOU BORN ON THE 23 (TWENTY THREE) OF ANY MONTH
THAN KINDLY READ THE FOLLOWING:

IF YOU WERE BORN ON THE 23rd

You are extremely independence, self-centered and sufficient. You may have an eccentricity for which you are known. You may be interested in art and music or new age ideals.

You have an interesting way of viewing life and turns events to your advantage. Verbal expression, witty, and, at times, defiant you can be petty and critical under stress. Generally however you excel in persuasion and know what other peoples will buy. You may appear youthful a long time. You are versatile and talented and there are few things you cannot do. You have a very sharp mind and a fine understanding of the body, which makes careers in medicine or health both possible and rewarding.

It also reveals how you can tackle the problems and challenges that come your way and also how you shall grab opportunities through the passage of your life. The birthday number is very closely connected to adaptability, which makes changes easier for you than for others. Your number relates to your inherent talents and abilities in you.

You have an easy path to good relationships with the result you generally get along well with most people you meet in life. You have a gift for communication and promoting yourself. You are quite charming affectionate and sensitive. You work well with others as long as there are not too many restrictions placed upon you. You do not like to be stacked to the same place for long; you easily get restless and bored if positioned at one and same situation for pretty long.

You are quite affectionate and sensitive. You work well with others as long as there are not too many restrictions placed upon you. You do not like to be cooped up in the same place for long; you get restless and bored easily. The independence of spirit, originality, fearlessness in thoughts, speech and expressions make you a fighter by nature. Your determination, self-confidence and courage in you are added by lively thinking and vigorous thoughts, which give you great success and recognition and you, are rewarded with this magnitude prize.

You have a very sharp mind and have gifted and promoted yourself with skills of communication and speech. You possess talent in verbal and writing skills, and this leads you to become excellent sales managers. Your challenge is to be willing to start your enterprise and take adequate steps toward enlarging it to its full scale. You are orderly and patient. You have a talent for seeing both the side details of a plan and how it should be worked and unfolded.

You have creative and witty nature which makes you to approach a problem methodically and systematically. Your solutions tend to be unique. You like not to be cheated as you are talented and there are very few things which you cannot do. You keep your own counsel and have much inner strength. On the reverse side, you can be nervous and may suffer grave doubts about yourself, which you also tend to hide in front of others.

People with Number 23 need to take any life situations wisely and sporty. They must do their best to stay away from any violent conflicts. As they are enthusiastic, ambitious people, looking for spiritual satisfaction in life must refrain themselves from any violence. Since they have a creative thinking, with sharp open-mind, and are quite imaginative and bold, this allows them to quickly implement their plans into reality. They take life seriously and firmly and they intend to take everything that is possible for them to work out.

They are not afraid of any obstacles. Usually they keep their emotions under control. They are very fair and merciful, and can tolerate the other types as well, because they are quite soft and curious they develop their skills in the right direction, they make a good career. if they sincerely believe that as to what they are doing is the right thing. At times they may be somewhat nervous, but and are able to restrain their passions. They possess many great talents. A good and harmonious relationship is quite possible for the Number 23 with two types of people: one those who will obey them, and the other who possess the powers of this kind, but the biggest appreciation they will always show for those, who really obey them.

Positive qualities: enthusiastic, ambitious people looking for spiritual satisfaction refraining themselves from any violence. Creative thinking, sharp open-mind, quite imaginative and bold.

Negative Traits: nervousness, suffer grave doubts about self, tend to hide in front of others. avoiding many restrictions, and self-centered person

# CHAPTER 24

## Numerology

Know About Your Self
Through Numerology

READ WHAT YOUR BIRTH NO HAS TO SAY ABOUT YOU

24 TWENTY FOURTH

IF YOU BORN ON THE 24 (TWENTY FOURTH) OF ANY MONTH
THAN KINDLY READ THE FOLLOWING:

IF YOU WERE BORN ON THE 24th

You want to build a family empire. You will be very unhappy alone or without domestic responsibilities. You love to accumulate wealth for yourself and others and will do well in traditional occupation such as teaching, accounting, banking, real estate. Your ideas were set earlier in life and will tend not to change.

You admire creative and spontaneous people and may be inclined to marry one (since you feel very secure with your own abilities). You consider yourself liberal and open; other may not. You may be very emotional or prone to jealousy. You are careful, cautious and productive. Most of your plan comes to fruition.

Your artistic talent goes in many directions you have a greater capacity for responsibility in helping others. You may also become the mediator and peacemaker in any kind of inharmonious condition or situations. Devoted to family and friends, you tend to manage and protect them. This added feature of yours adds to the emotional nature and perhaps to your sensitivities. Love for other and affections are important to you both while giving and while receiving important advice.

You can be a bit impractical overly emotional impractical, and melodramatic. You have the habit to magnify your heart breaking issues. Your sympathetic nature may cause you to interfere in other's affairs and get you into trouble, especially when they involve in some kind of criticism with you. You need others to give you sound advice. You are a good friend and a faithful companion.

You are willingly to provide a soft ear to hear, or lend a good shoulder to cry on. This quality of yours attracts distressed people to you who gladly rely upon you looking at your talents. You being responsible and helpful are willing to sacrifice much to maintain harmony in important relationships on somebody's call.

Although you are energetic, you must know your limits. At the same time, you must avoid being taken advantage of or being be fooled by others. You are gifted in acting and drama. You also do well in business, because, you are careful patient and systematic, in your approach as your artistic talent goes in many directions, generally do succeed in all matters relating to business affairs.it may also be possible for you to get big chances to be a top leader and have huge number of followers.

People with number 24 as their number can do any business from Import—Export to trading of, Garments, Real Estate, and any line with deals with commission. They will shine as excellent sales person to mediators for all kinds of business disputes.

These people are in general hard workers, creative designers, social reformers, and also possess the quality to attract people and influence them immensely. They are very brave at heart and possess magnetic eyes to attract masses. One can see the very look of their glowing eyes and say that these people are ruled by the planet Venus.

Their mind always desires for beautiful things, like acting, dance poetry and music. To live a blissful life will be their prime ambition; all worldly Pleasures will lure them very much. They never get intimated by failures rather they will bounce back with great force. Their appearances will be attractive. They will be one of the luckiest people among other numbers in numerology. They will be blessed with money and fame in their life.

Number 24 born are the ones this world would witness as musicians, painters, artists, actors and singers. They draw the masses with their attractive physical form; this makes them very popular in their field. On the reverse side of other coin they are calm stature, peace loving and kind one such person who will possess supernatural like qualities of love and forgiveness and their physical structure will be sharp like of a warrior.

If their planetary position of their governing planet is weak they become threat to a society, such Person will fall prey to greed, enmity, and would become, lustful person, dishonest persons and cheats. Such people will attract others and exploit them with their beauty or false projection of them. In order to nullify their weak points their weak planetary planets need to be treated for remedies.

Numerology often speak of women who are born with number 24 having weak planet Venus in their birth chart loves to enjoy their lives and live in luxury enjoying all the worldly pleasures at any cost. Such women usually get married to rich man who fulfills their desire. But if they don't get wealthy partner then they sometimes even get into amoral activities to fulfill their desires and wishes. It is advisable to name a 24 born child according to her /his birth number.

Positive qualities: love for beautiful things, like acting, dance poetry and music. Excellent sales person to mediators for all kinds of business disputes. Liking for occupation such as teaching, accounting, banking, real estate Musicians, painters, artists, actors and singers

Negative Traits: If their ruling planet Venus is fall into amoral activities, greed, enmity, and would become, lustful person or dishonest persons false projection

# CHAPTER 25

## Numerology

Know About Your Self
Through Numerology

READ WHAT YOUR BIRTH NO HAS TO SAY ABOUT YOU

25 TWENTY FIFTH

IF YOU BORN ON THE 25 (TWENTY FIFTH) OF ANY MONTH
THAN KINDLY READ THE FOLLOWING:

IF YOU WERE BORN ON THE 25th

You are very intuitive and impressionable and must guard against emotional instability through the intensity of your emotion. You may be hard for others to understand. You can be extremely talented in artistic or musical fields and have great rapport to animals.

You may even choose to be a veterinarian. Three may be difficult times (especially around ages 27 and 28) when you will find some type of therapy valuable in assisting your personal growth. There may be a bisexual nature. Do not cut yourself off from family and friends when you are feeling melancholy. Find a stable diet and exercise routine.

Your number 25 makes you dream of big projects it also does not support you with action. As you move ahead you dream of another big enterprise and once again you miss your bus. This happen of because of the initial vibrating numbers 2 and number 5. This combination leads you to flirt with attractive ladies but you here too you do not go any further. The fair sex gets attracted to you, but they find you unsure of yourself due to a faulty number and your name. Your love seems to succeed but again slips through your hands.

You have keen interest and investigation and research subjects but your analytical skill forces you to avoid taking any risk at its face value. This is where you are at your best. You deeply understand the matter at hand, and then make sound and good decisions. You would fare well in the field of psychology, philosophy teaching.

Your main issues are that while you are using your mind to study and analyze your life's issues, you are prone to neglect or dismiss your heart for which you can easily become imbalanced and which can make you aloof, critical, and even depressed. Do not allow your intellect powers to rule your life to such a point that it obscures qualities of understanding, compassion, love and affection.

You don't share your feelings so easily. You prefer to work alone and choose your own path. You have the neck to finish projects once commenced. You possess excellent artistic talent, especially in painting art and sculpture.

You are very sensitive and feel deeply involved in anything you do, but you do not communicate them well. If you work hard to develop this skill and maintain deep and maintain important relationships you are sure to succeed. You must learn to share your emotions and deeper thoughts. Trust would be the key to your emotional live and happiness.

You possess special interest in science, technical, scientific, or other difficult subjects. You may become perfectionist and a follower for details. Your thinking is often logical rational and intuitive, and you share responsibility. Your feelings may run deep trouble, but you are not very likely to show them. You are more of a private person, more introspective and perhaps more inflexible. In friendships you are very cautious and reserved.

You are probably inventive, and given to unique approaches and solutions. You have a sound, rational mind and a fine insight vision. You are basically a logical and intellectual person with fine intuition, which, and a good listener which guides you well through life. You are capable of investigating and researching subjects deeply.

People born on 25th of a month are deep into religion, spirituality, and the metaphysics. They find and explore the spirituality in the roots of mantras and they practice what it takes them to reach spiritual heights but at the same time they cannot leave everything and become a saintly person. Their body is blessed with natural energies which creates strong magnetic field around them and thus making them to experience many spiritual powers.

You can be seen and judged as a dignified person, would like to dress elegantly and project yourself as a clean and tidy person. Your facial outlook is attractive and most of you are tall and handsome. Twenty fifth born people are not chatter box but the every word they utter will be after proper analysis and thinking. When they are with highly confident then you can see them talking un interrupt nonstop about any topic given to them, but when they are in low confidence they can be even be compared to a mute and dull person.

Another common factor of these people are short temper, most of them are known for their bad temperament and anger. They long for solitude more than human bonding, Happiness or sorrow they prefer to enjoy it in solitude manner rather than to share it with others.

These people also develop great passion for fine arts and turn on to become a legend in that particular field. They are highly patriotic and their devotion towards their nation is quite high; they are inclined to their traditional habits customs and roots. They won't easily go or many changes.

One of the sad things about 25 born is their marital life. Not often they get the woman they like or want to get married to. Their marriage is often fruitless and they prefer to live by force or compulsion. They live with their spouses for their own sake and for the sake of following the culture or society. It is seen that these people are seldom blessed with a good wives. Another saddening thing about them is that don't follow others, but they create their own rules and path and their life will flows according to the numerological significance of this number.

Positive qualities: Fine thoughts, accurate analysis, good mind, specialists in finding the truth, deep understanding, scientific nature, religion follower, fine teacher and a true perfectionist.

Negative Traits: Does not trust anyone; highly introvert self-centered side, overly critical and intolerant. Works alone, lack emotion. You do not earn a good name in profession. a miser. You do not wear modern clothes and you don't wear any custom jewelers. Your money lies idle in the bank

# CHAPTER 26

## Numerology

Know About Your Self
Through Numerology

READ WHAT YOUR BIRTH NO HAS TO SAY ABOUT YOU

26 TWENTY SIXTH

IF YOU BORN ON THE 26 (TWENTY SIXTH) OF ANY MONTH
THAN KINDLY READ THE FOLLOWING:

IF YOU WERE BORN ON THE 26th

You are much less intense then the 17. You have a strong emotional capacity and love nature. Harmony is very important to you. You will be oriented towards marriage as much as work. You love to dress well, have a fine house, and well brought up children (for which you take credit). You are the more generous Eight.

You may brood about the past, hanging on to old arguments and beliefs. You may have big ideas, but want to include others to help you as you may not be as self-confident as the other Eight. You are more introspective and psychologically analytic.

You might consider a catering business, diplomacy, or administrative work in the social science.

Number twenty six people turn out to be very good professionals and are good in promoting themselves as leaders. Their and practical approach helps them in getting their followers very easily. They get into the pros and cons of every situation. They have a good sense of money and a talent for business. Their approach to business is original, creative and daring. They possess sound judgment of whatever you are doing. They seek to be a good managers and organizers. They are efficient and can handle large projects, enterprises, or businesses. Their specialty is that they are a realist, self-confident, practical, and highly ambitious, very diplomatic and tactful. They prefer to get things done by persuasion rather than force.

They are also dependable and have high expectations of themselves. They have a need for status and may show off the fruits of their work or labor with an impressive car or house. They can easily overdo such ostentatiousness, and may appear showy in the eyes of others.

Natives with 26th as their birthday of the month tend to modify their life path by increasing their capacity and capability to function accurately. They succeed in the business world as they are embarked with the powers of good organizational, managerial, and administrative traits and abilities. They are quite sufficient to handle money well. Being adaptable, cooperative, ambitious and energetic, they have a wonderful combination of being good to all and are known to be more practical, realistic and talented personalities.

Their challenge is to maintain a balance between their material goals and the fundamental qualities of understanding, compassion and love. Their immense lust for business life can cause them to become jealous and inimical toward others. They have strong character, but may be domineering and bossy. On the reverse side they have little patience with weakness, be it their own or someone else's. They need to be careful not to be discouraged too easily.

Numerology meanings for 26 suggest that they will have a stormy love life. The charms they have by give them good love compatibility. Irrespective of this charm and fascination they have to face a lot of enemies in their love life. That might sound funny, but actually number 26 gives lifetime adventures, travels and life threatening incidents, mysterious journey of life in search of quest.

People with this number may face grave dangers in all walks of life but they will somehow trick and overcome these dangers and live a normal life. Their passage to life is likely to be full of interesting events and risks. They will have some super natural powers and mystic qualities which would save them from all the dangers.

More or less to say their nature will help them in all ways to make sure their journey of life is safe. They have a great gift from nature which helps them in mysterious ways. If these persons study occult sciences, then they can even become Healers with power to cure.

Positive qualities: natural powers, mystic qualities, adaptable, cooperative, ambitious and energetic, good organizational, managerial, and administrative traits and abilities can handle large projects, enterprises, or businesses, self-confident, practical, and highly ambitious, very diplomatic and tactful

Negative Traits: immense lust for business, jealous and inimical toward others, false impressive nature, a lot of enemies in their love life.

# CHAPTER 27

## Numerology

Know About Your Self
Through Numerology

READ WHAT YOUR BIRTH NO HAS TO SAY ABOUT YOU

27 TWENTY SEVENTH

IF YOU BORN ON THE 27 (TWENTY SEVENTH) OF ANY MONTH
THAN KINDLY READ THE FOLLOWING:

IF YOU WERE BORN ON THE 27th

You are quieter than other Nines, but a keen observer of life. You may have musical or artistic ability and will yearn for distant places; you enjoy the poetry of the East, perhaps wish to be a member of an eastern religious community. You would make an excellent journalist, wild life photographer, calligrapher, or antique dealer.

You have many talents and interests, which can take a while to find. You are generous and forgiving of friends. To be happy and fulfilled, you need to have an ideal to follow. You are always learning about letting go.

You are a strong bold, courageous and determined person. Because of your fighting nature and can overcome strife and opposition. You care, love and respect yourself even if others do not agree and oppose you. You would love to have control over your own destiny. With this you can easily be a great commander and leader. You are also a kind humane person; you will never leave your friends behind. You always want to help others. You are deeply connected with your family and home and you always want to make them happy.

Number 27 natives are very caring and generous, giving away their last dollar to help. With their charm they have no problem making friends and nobody is a stranger to them. They have so many different personalities that people around them have a hard time understanding them. They are like chameleons, ever changing and blending in.

They have tremendous luck, but also can suffer from extremes in fortune and mood. To be successful they need to build a loving foundation. When they take up a work, they will struggle hard to complete it perfectly. They can work all the time without taking rest. Since they are much interested in sensual pleasures they are quite careful as not to offend anybody.

Some of them may be dull in imagining while some others think and imagine with lightning speed. On the reverse side of it they have a rude nature and get caught with unnecessary trouble. Their mind is drawn towards all kind of pleasures. They are eager to buy and collect luxury articles. They are ill fond of machines, vehicles and buildings. They get mental peace from looking at natural scenery and regions.

Natives born on the 27th of the month are are governed by number 9 and that is their ruling number. There are certain positive traits associated with 27 as they reduce to a single digit number 9, hence there is a need to look beyond the basics of this number to see if there's any real significance stored in it. They represent the concept of major transitions cycles. While learning and letting go and moving forward all positive parts of life, transitions are highly charged, and at times it can be too much for some to handle these transition cycles. When these natives are faced with something that's unknown and makes them uncomfortable, they may divert themselves to drugs and alcohol to cope up with these harsh cycles. Some may even, seek a way out through suicide, or engage in reckless behavior that ends up crossing the limits.

Born on 27th day of the month adds a taste of selflessness and humanitarianism to life passage. Those are the ones who can work very well with people, but at the same time they need a good bit of time to rest and meditate. With your this number, there is a very positive human nine and philanthropic approach in most of things that you think and do. This birthday helps you to be broadminded, tolerant, generous and cooperative. You are the type of person who uses persuasion rather than force to achieve your ends. You tend to be very sensitive to others' needs and feelings, and you able to give much in the way of friendship without expecting a lot in return.

This also adds that you are broad-minded and educated in several different fields, particularly the arts and mystic science. Many great artists and talented people are found under this number. You may be a late starter and would take to take some time before choosing a profession. You would some greater experience and exposure before you find the one area in which you will excel.

You can be compared to man people in different walks of life. You will often be traveling and thus go through many changes in life through this travel. You dream of humanity. You also like to improve the conditions of people, whether they are of your community, state, or your country. This is where you get satisfied and your deepest satisfaction lies performing some useful task for others to benefit. Thus are the most important and fortunate soul which possess the highest wisdom, and which is full of knowledge. Such souls will discover love within itself and will not search others for their love and wisdom.

Number 27 is far more spiritually inclined. Both 9 and 27 are highly praised numbers. But having name number 72 is very rare, hence 27 is mostly considered beneficial. There are many hidden greatness behind number 27. Only few options of greatness have been explored and the rest are still open to discovery. Yes for sure, this is the number of Saints and enlightened beings. People with this name number cannot do a unlawful or sinful act purposefully, or even if they happen to do, they pay the price in their this life only. Spiritual powers or yogic powers are very much possible for them. They could be masters in Numerology, Meditation, Astrology, Palmistry, Telepathy and healing touch. This number has a power to break ones wheel of life and death itself. People experience karmic effects of previous lives in this life itself and attain liberation, or they would have been born as saints to serve the humanity.

Positive Trends: creative expression, friendly and spiritual, congenial, humanitarian, fine instincts, forgiving nature, obligations, and does good works, artistic and superb writing talents.

Negative Trends: possessiveness of unknown things makes them uncomfortable, they may divert themselves to drugs and alcohol, selflessness, scattered interests, moodiness, careless with money matters and big finances.

# CHAPTER 28

## Numerology

Know About Your Self
Through Numerology

READ WHAT YOUR BIRTH NO HAS TO SAY ABOUT YOU

28 TWENTY EIGHT

IF YOU BORN ON THE 28 (TWENTY EIGTH) OF ANY MONTH
THAN KINDLY READ THE FOLLOWING:

IF YOU BORN ON THE 28th

You love your independence and freedom and yet are much more loving and affectionate than other ones. You love to be the center of attraction with people that you admire and respect. You always have quality friends.

Your mate will have to be a strong person in his/her own right. And you will never settle for less than your ideal. Like all ones you are an executive capable of sacrificing for your ambition. You would be successful in any profession, especially teaching, law engineering, architecture, and design. You have dramatic flair in you all do and will chose a mate who shares this trait.

You tend to attain success in a very short span of time, but in the end you often lose everything. Apart from that, you will suffer heavy losses due to friends and relatives. Losses will either be monetary or non-monetary. When you give credit to anyone, you can hardly expect to get back the same. Money would not be given back to them. This number generally is opted as not so lucky number.

People with number come up with new ideas and execute them in the natural way. Having things to be done in their own way is another label that gets them treated as being stubborn and arrogant. Twenty eights are extremely honest and do well to learn some diplomacy skills. They like to take the initiative and are often leaders or bosses. Being self-employed is definitely helpful for them.

This number 28 comprises of the three energies and vibrations of the numbers 2, 8, and 1. The number two is the energy of the number this makes the person sensitive but the 8 energy sees a drive for success. Together they give the attributes of leadership. The 28 is a stubborn and independent energy. They will excel anywhere they can show their leadership qualities.

Natives with birth no twenty eight like anything which are luxurious and which makes them powerful and successful. These people appreciate all type of power tools, a bottle of brandy or wine, or a top-of-the-range barbeque. Women love champagne, a box of their favorite chocolates, a subscription to their favorite magazine, or a voucher for a day spa and massage. 28 Day Number would make debater a nice jockey host or salesperson.

Natives born on the 28th day of the month add a special tone liberty and independence like a time for giving birth and a time for dying, a time for planting of seeds time for uprooting what has been planted. This unique quality also speaks of the time to kill and heal, time to destroy and build, time to cry and laugh, and finally a time to mourn and dance. These people have the capacity to know how to throw stones away and to gather them, to embrace anything and to refrain from embracing.

A birthday on the 28th of any month gives greater will power and self-confidence, unlike others This birthday is one that powers with the ability to start a job and continue to finished it till end. These natives may prefer to use a wider angle. Though they are sensitive, but their feeling stay somewhat depressed.

Other added special qualities of number twenty are highly emotional independent, idealistic and are extremely ambitious. They are excellent planners, with a talent for directing and managing groups of people. On the reverse side, they become irritated and angry easily, and are given to laughter and tantrums. Their positive traits are that they are highly creative and have a great mind for marshalling facts in order to sell ideas. You make a wonderful salesperson. With your determination and inventive mind, you have potential for achievement in getting much financial success.

Positive Trends: Leader, organizer, inventive mind masculine body, creative, Courageous and strong

Negative Trends: Selfish Domineering, Impulsive Arrogant Aggressive Obstinate Self-Centered Pompous Bossy Insensitive

# CHAPTER 29

## Numerology

Know About Your Self
Through Numerology

READ WHAT YOUR BIRTH NO HAS TO SAY ABOUT YOU

29 TWENTY NINTHE

IF YOU BORN ON THE 29 (TWENTY NINE) OF ANY MONTH
THAN KINDLY READ THE FOLLOWING:

IF YOU BORN ON THE 29th

If your birthday is on the twenty ninth of any month, you are highly intuitive and creative. Your spiritual interest is generally heightened. Your number adds up too eleven which is the master number of inspiration in the mystical spiritual world. Like the11, you need to stay grounded by activities that offer discipline and immediate reward (such as working in the garden, cooking, sewing, building).

You will have to watch your moods and know what to do before they get out of hand. You may be an inspiration to others and may attract the lime light through teaching or your art. You can also find success in occupations such as accounting and waiting tables, while pursuing your artistic interest. If a women, you may be very pretty, or as a man you have rather gentlemanly features. You also possess leadership abilities. Your mind thinks in pictures. Your intuition makes you a wonderful counselor and healer. When you are in a dark mood you get depressed easily due to the lack of confidence.

You are polite, modest and diplomatic. You love beauty and harmony and you have the ability to persuade, and at times can be quite forceful. You log in to social attention. At times you can be very emotional, often in the gates of happiness and sadness. You are sensitive and easily influenced by your surroundings this making you to easily get hurt. You have a special talent of inspiring people. Many people admire you without your knowing the truth of it. You sense your wisdom. You have fine mind keen insights and you to lead your life by inspiration, rather by calculated reflections. You are imaginative and creative and your intuition is your god's gift. You seem to draw information and ideas from out of the sky. You are also driven by spiritual pursuits that no matter what you do in life, the world of spirit and philosophy will be central to your daily events. You are very aware and sensitive, with outstanding intuitive skills and analytical abilities adds a tone of idealism to your nature.

Natives of number 29 often suffer from nervous tension. They would only work quite well with the people of the same number. This number belongs to the number 2 in numerology with this effect they believe less in peace and ahimsa. They start a fight in some way or the other, would play pranks or start a quarrel with someone unknown or known to them. They are generally termed as fighter cocks. They don't usually trust anyone. They very insecure in most part of their life. These folks keep on thinking whom to trust and whom not to trust and often complaint that their best and good friends have cheated or deceived them. They

117

generally boast of courage, but in reality they are quite timid and fearful but rather most uncomfortable. There is a great amount of fear in them, and their morality is not true in their public life. If somebody dare them or stand against them then they get afraid and retreat, but if they find that the person is weak, then they will prowl on them and intimidate them.

With the influence of the planet moon twenty nine born natives mostly complain about one thing or the other and they never settle for things so easily. Their minds are very wavering and unstable due to the supreme effect of this planet. Women too are very jealous, short tempered, and envy others. People born on 29 are liable to get into the bad habits or bad friendship, and they must refrain themselves from these false temptations to reach a good place in life. When the planet moon's effect is bad these people can become extremely violent and dangerous. During trouble times, when they are emotional or sad, they themselves fall to prey about suicide or ending life. This type of nature is often seen in category two people.

The positive side of number 29 born is that they possess abundance creativity, originality, intuition, and the power of argumentation. The career best suitable for them are arts, entertainment, lawyers, here they can intensely use their positive energies to attain higher status in society. They are very good actors, and can also excel in TV and film industry.

As they have the habit and tendency to argue very long, they can be at their best in becoming a lawyer. Even women born on twenty ninth must try to control their temper during full moon days.

These natives are in possession of spiritual strength, since their life is filled with uncertainties, deception from unreliable friends, unexpected dangers and considerable grief caused by the opposite sex the spiritual power in them, saves them from all uncertainties. This number is also an indication and warning to them in the area of their personal career and life. If it happens to be a compound number the name need to be changed in the spelling to get them lifted out this vibrating force. If 29 is the birth number, it must be made to dilute and to neutralize, or erase this karmic burden by choosing a new name (or spelling) with a strongly positive compound key number.

They need to remember that the development of absolute faith in goodness and the absolute power of the Self and with the constant and energetic cultivation of optimism will help them to act as a remedial medicine for the problems of their life.

If they have learned to accept troubles, and have also learned not to blame others or seek revenge for the bad that they have suffered they will have to change their name number to a powerful number which will change their destiny and make them a happen person in their lives.

Positive Trends: Strong, Feminine, Sensitive, Friendly, Companionship, Tactful, Peacemaker, Kind, Thoughtful, Psychic, Cooperative, Reflective, Creative, Communication, Diplomatic, Adaptable, Rhythmic, Gentle, Harmonious, Receptive, Considerate

Negative trends: Unforgiving, Indecisive. Dependent, pitiable, Emotional, sensitive, non-co-operative Carelessness, Strident Tactless, Extremist, Dishonest. Must accept troubles.

# CHAPTER 30

## Numerology

Know About Your Self
Through Numerology

READ WHAT YOUR BIRTH NO HAS TO SAY ABOUT YOU

30 THIRTH

IF YOU BORN ON THE 30 (THIRTH) OF ANY MONTH
THAN KINDLY READ THE FOLLOWING:

IF YOU WERE BORN ON THE 30th

You have exceptional high energy. Your enthusiasm is infectious; you can motivate and persuade others. You are outspoken and have a flair for having just the right word or fact to win a argument. You may have strong psychic ability.

You would be an excellent teacher, actor, or musician. You would make a wonderful minister. You are serious and intense about what interest you, but will find it difficult to fulfill old promises. Like other Threes, you are flirtatious. Guard against a tendency to drink too much or overspend on cloths and socializing.

Yet another vital point in your business should be not to have your business name or product name, or brand name as multiple of 3 which is six. You must also avoid the days ruled by number six as it may prove to be unlucky for you. In such events you have to correct your name in some other vibrating number and moreover you have to change your name with some numerology compatibility. You have to do it in a new name number that signifies progress prosperity and wealth in business.

Since most people live in predominantly, the materialistic world, they will not like to have their name number as thirty. This being one of the most underrated numbers, many people don't even know the greatness of it. A truly altruistic in nature is what one can describe about name number 30. It is a fabulous number for selfless service and devotion to humanity the usual diplomacy and cunning. On the contrary people they usually lead a thoughtful life, possess great wisdom of mind.

These natives are best suited to be public speakers for a religious organization. They will also be talented in writing and poetry. Many well-known authors, story tellers and poets have name number 30, where most number of authors, poets, creative geniuses belongs. People with name number 30 should be cautious of diseases related to bones and nervous system.

Your birthday on the thirtieth day of the month shows individual self-expression is necessary for your happiness. You tend to have a good way of expressing yourself with words, certainly in a manner that is clear and understandable. You have a good chance of success in fields requiring skill with words.

This number also adds to the quality that you can be very dramatic in your presentation and you and a good actor or a natural mimic. You have a vivid imagination that can assist you in becoming a good lyrist or script writer or a good story-teller. Strong in your opinions, you always tend to think you are on the right side of an issue.

You are a good salesperson. You are good at love friendly, affectionate and social. You are imaginative, possess creative talent and are extra witted. You are an artist at heart. You excel in visuals, writing, and performing arts. You are charismatic and have great enthusiasm apart from being charming. You have a fine sense of harmony in everything that you do from your style of dress to the way you decorate your home. You have a gift with plants and flower arranging. You make a wonderful interior designer and a fine cook.

Being moody and bit lethargic you may be subjected to rapid ups and downs in life. You can waste your talent in too much social gatherings socializing and may not enough be focused and disciplined in your life. You need bit of advice as to be careful and not to waste time and energy on petty matters. Hence you are also advised to keep your long-term priorities in a positive perspective view.

Positive Trends:
Positive Characteristics: talented imaginative, expressive artists. Tolerant, joyful, optimistic, inspiring, jovial, youthful, dynamic.

Negative Characteristics: 30's are often vain, extravagant and prone to complaining. Intolerance, hypocrisy, impatience and superficiality.

# CHAPTER 31

## Numerology

Know About Your Self
Through Numerology

READ WHAT YOUR BIRTH NO HAS TO SAY ABOUT YOU

31 THIRTY ONE

IF YOU BORN ON THE 31 (THIRTY ONE) OF ANY MONTH
THAN KINDLY READ THE FOLLOWING:

IF YOU WERE BORN ON THE 31st

You derive great satisfaction from working with your hands and may be a sculptor or painter. You may have very high ambition for yourself. You are very traditional love your friends and remember their birthdays.

You may be a great cook. You love to travel and socialize, but work for extremely long hours if motivated. You do not enjoy living alone and will take on solicitous attitude towards your mate. You love talk about yourself and your plans and expected others to be interested.

You are an excellent care taker organizer and manager. You have a great love for your community. You would follow family tradition and community rules. You are the foundation stone of any enterprise. You are dependable and quite an energetic worker. You possess a good amount of talent that is searching for concrete forms of expression. You can work hard, long and continuously. As long as you tend to take good care of yourself, you have excellent power of concentration and vision.

You love travel and don't like to live alone. For this you should marry quite early for the sake of responsibility and stability. You being practical thinker with strong imagination you often show success in the business matter. Being sincere and serious you possess, patience and determination necessary to accomplish great heights.

The keys to your success are your willingness and your sincere hard work. Your fellows recognize your discipline and come to trust and rely upon you in order to maintain order and discipline in their life, and for the most opportunities that come in their lives. Basically, you may feel that you have yet to find the work you truly love or were meant to do. There may be a feeling that your talents are buried too deep for you to find them. This can lead you to try many different vocations without a feeling that you have truly found your place.

The stars and this universe guide you always. But you need to cultivate faith and willingness in yourself. If you refuse to develop such an attitude, you may wander from place to place, job to job, friendship to friendship relationship to relationship. Therefore you must use your considerable perseverance and determination.

You do not care about materialistic possessions or gains, about the money losses or the superficial profits; it's the freedom of speech and action that you care most. Freedom to do all things at will is your main desire.

Number 31 are the people who act according to their own will and heart, and they happen not get into any sort of thing which acts against their mental happiness even if the all the thing are of good lucrative attraction. They enjoy deep research and studies of human psychology, Astrology, religious scriptures and occult sciences.

If the natives of number 31 do not care for the good vibrating number matching their birth no and keep any name accordingly to their wish and will they are likely to lead a goalless wanderlust,

Vagabond life. In this way, they are become the real rebels in their own society who defy the traditions and social practices. Even if success comes on their way, they don't cherish it or embrace it with passion but to the contrary, they will nonattached and uninterested. Hence forth non matching number should be avoided in their own interest.

Their skill will help them to raise their own status in life and with this unique skill they would be helping the people by knowledge of scriptures, science and mathematics. They desire to be as free, as a bird and so they do not like to live under the control of others. They know something about everything. They will express their ideas bluntly through speech and writing. People will seek their advice.

They are prone to lust and they often visit various places for the sake of gathering the knowledge of competitive skill. In this way, they enrich themselves with wide experience. During a conversation, they will wait till the other person completes his speech but will tend to interfere.

When provoked and they become angry at once. But as they grow older with the year to come, they will gather some experience and will improve themselves. Whatever it may be, they are not deterred by worries. For a short while they may feel sad but soon they will drive out the shady thoughts.

Natives having number 31 as their number have high nervous power. They are quite tall and their looks are majestic. They have good power of wisdom and talented thoughts.

They are seen helping others and with all these qualities they are praised by one and all. If anyone sheds tears narrating his difficulty, these people feel proud in joining him. They have an extremely sharp brain and are capable of replying at lightning speed. They are welcomed everywhere. They would not become addicted to any bad habit. Even if they happen to get into this, they have the power to give it up soon.

They would strain themselves to collect and earn and money. But when they want to spend it, with a merry heart their tension starts and this leads to unhappiness. When alone, they will feel sorry for their spending and extravagance. Though they are mentally bold yet they are stubborn and rigid. This behavior can, often, lead to frustration and repression for them. Things seem to take for better especially when they leave their rigidity.

It is generally not good if your name number does not contribute to find worldly enjoyments or worldly success. This will lead you to be a poor husband or parent. You must examine your name properly to see if it does contain any bad alphabet. Bad combination of alphabets in your number can cause you loss, defamation, and accidents. Hence forth the power of numbers advises you to avoid negative numerology in your name.

Positive Traits: quite tall and their looks are majestic master builder scale solving. strong leader, well practical approach, the idealist, charisma to attract.

Negative Traits: stubborn and rigid, undertakings unorthodox approaches to problems, unnecessary,spending, extravagant.

# CHAPTER 32

## Numerology

Know About Your Self
Through Numerology

READ WHAT YOUR BIRTH NO HAS TO SAY ABOUT YOU

DOUBLE DIGITS NUMBERS
COMPOUND NUMBERS

**A** double-digit number or a compound number is s the mixture or combination of two single digit number and its characteristics are mostly dominated by that of a single digit number that it represents.

The dual number highlights certain aspects, of the two single digit numbers but it never eliminates any aspect completely. For example number ten highlights the leadership ability of a 1, number 30 is lead of 3, and a 60 is a high trend of number 6. A short explanation of double-digit numbers from number ten to number ninety nine are given below:

To find your dual digit number, let us take the total of the letters in your name before you reduce them to a single digit. The ultimate meaning of the double-digit numbers is given in detail:

Number 10 indicate all the qualities of that of number 1. It shows the person is powerful leader, sharply focused in his thoughts and nature and is Stream lined for success. This person can be ruthless in the persuasion of his aim and goals. He can become a dominating and angry tyrant.

Number 11: Highly intuitive, psychic, sub-conscious and the conscious mind, highly charged. can be at times neurotic.

Number 12 It is highly creative, individualistic, and unconventional. Represents the interests self-centered

Number 13 :Hard work and slow progress, difficult but rewarding down-to-earth. Reliable, trustworthy, rigid and lacking a sense of humor.

Number14: Wild streaks. Changing attitude and adventurous, capability to destroy, lack of focus and commitment, trouble shooter. Guard against self-indulgence.

Number15: Loving, forgiving, and extremely tolerant, responsible, successful, dynamic, and strong. travel, adventure, and experimentation. This number can bring self-relent.

Number 16: Difficultly faced, especially during the early part of life. Great potential, spiritual growth and self-knowledge. Self-destructive.

Number 17 It is spiritual growth, faith, and balance. It is also wealth or bankruptcy. It is an inner struggle to remain true to spiritual and moral values.

Number 18: Spiritual, International Business specialist, disparity between idealism and selfishness, lacking consciousness.

Number 19: Strong and individualistic. Self-reliant and confident, bring loneliness, qualities of a leader and bullish.

Number 20: Sensitive, intuitive, vulnerable to criticism, generates emotional problems weakness and cowardice in case of challenges.

Number:21 Procrastinate. Individualistic, and unconventional and intuitive.

Number:22 demanding and obsessive, living on edge. Progressive. Need to devote self to something larger than life.

Number 23: Unrealistic, surrendered, people lover, freedom fighter, a promoter of causes.

Number 24: domestic struggles and divorce, counsels and comforts others. It likes music, particularly rhythm.

Number 25: Spiritual leader. Lover of group endeavors. too serious. great difficulty in sharing feelings with others.

Number 26: Excellent in business and management. a good strategist, workaholic, often disorganized in personal affairs.

Number 27: Counselor, volunteer, an artist, successful, inheritance nature. rigid and narrow-minded.

Number 28: Ruthless, dominating and angry compassion and intolerance.

Number 29 : high sensitivity, imaginative and creative powers, More serious and less social.

Number 30: Humorous, communication skill, creativity. jovial, superficial.

Number 31: more extrovert and fun-loving, more creative and unfaithful.

Number 32: moody, sensitive, up and down emotionally,

Number 33: Self-sacrifice, dependent, teacher. Comfort ability to other. and compulsive liar.

Number 34: intelligent. Spirituality and purity. Sharing with others, strong warrior.

Number 35: Freelancer, business adviser cum creative—inventor, gadget-designer, socialite, but does not work well with others.

Number 36: Creativeness, genius. self-consciousness, inhibited, aloofness.

Number 37: individualistic, a scholar, a voracious reader, excellent imagination, often disorganized.

Number 38: more realistic. Very intuitive, not a good admitter, earning through sale of art or antiques. Generates phobias.

Number 39: Functional art. good in acting and dancing. Problems in rejection and separation.

Number 40: organized, systematic, and methodical. Critical of others, intolerant, and sometimes prejudicial.

Number 41: capable of directing energies to many different projects successfully. selfish, has a lack of humor, and is sometimes criminal.

Number 42: Insensitive, political aspirations. Administrator works in government institutions.

Number 43: Inferiority complex, good concentration, best perfectionism, frustrations, and feeling of inferiority.

Number 44: Good for business, military career a visional and a doer. Great potentiality.

Number 45: banking, or international institutions. Not comfortable with self. Cynical.

Number 46: It represents leadership (see 10), and is often tactless and rude. It is always well prepared and confident.

Number 47: inner struggle between practical, down to earth spiritual balancer, achiever, it is a prophet and counselor extraordinaire.

Number 48: a visionary planner. lost in unrealistic dreams.

Number 49: caretaker makes effort for others. Problem-solver. be a hero and a friend to everyone.

Number 50: A high octave of 5. Freedom-loving, versatile. Open to new ideas, willing to take a chance. Possess sexual hang-ups.

Number 51: It is more independent and aggressive.

Number 52: creative intuitive sensitive and clever.

Number 53: business-oriented. more verbal, creative, and intelligent

Number 54: less organized and disciplined, difficulty in finishing projects. Dreamer and idealistic.

Number 55: It is extremely freedom-loving, and likes to travel. social, selfish lonely. success in sales.

Number 56: extreme sensitivity, balance, a desire for freedom with an equally, strong desire to be part of a family

Number 57: intelligence inventiveness creative and unconventional wisdom late in life,.

Number 58: opinionated hard worker, successful. Opportunist, fine decision maker and dogmatic.

Number 59: very persuasive convincing. successful lawyers and fundraisers. uncanny ability with people diverse cultures.

Number 60: loving, caring, responsible. brings subservience.

Number 61: Problems in love relationships. In need of family and friends demanding, secretive; researchers, law officers,

Number 62: medical field less sensitive, caretaker.

Number 63: unfriendly, less outgoing. sexually promiscuous.

Number 64: un comfort ability un—organized and more creative.

Number 65: freedom and domestic affairs brings a criminal tendency.

Number 66: Generous to a fault, financial ups and downs. Loyal, loving. Successful in itself.

Number 67: analytical intelligence creativity. Inventors and mathematicians.

Number 68: Good in business, insensitive, very loyal. sense of humor.

Number 69: teachers, Creativeness, self-sacrificing activists medical professionalisms.

Number 70: loner, truth knowledge seeker Intelligence, originality. eccentric.

Number 71: less authoritative a loner.

Number 72: an excellent conversationalist, voracious reader.

Number 73: independent likes to work alone. demanding in relationships.

Number 74 bad eating habits and disorder, premonitions and intense dreams.

Number 75: more analytical and less creative.

Number 76: management or organization. turn ideas into reality. dogmatism and religious fanaticism.

Number 77: most intelligent and inventive of all numbers. It also represents spiritual wisdom.

Number 78: struggle between the spiritual and the material. make and lose fortunes.

Number 79: Political and spiritual leaders concern for mankind, be ruthless and self-righteous.

Number 80: good businessmen. In management personals in military, entrepreneurs, lack of independence. It is an extravert number.

Number 81: money-oriented. lacks spiritual understanding. brings violence.

Number 82: leadership and courage. survivor. lack of stability in marriage. never get married or get married many times.

Number 83: more business-oriented and less sensitive and vulnerable.

Number 84: Little less in organization and quite visionary.

Number 85: trendy and bullish nature. masculine in figure,

Number 86: more self-oriented. Irresponsible self-indulgent.

Number 87: practical good in money handling struggle spiritual and the material thoughts.

Number 88: contradictions. business, not good for relationships. It is insensitive.

Number 89: aristocrat much travel. difficult for a person to be alone, even for a short period of time.

Number 90 respected by many self-sacrificing and humble. positive nature. likes to be aloof,.

Number 91: success in career, creative fields, unable to handle huge money.

Number 92: great concern for mankind.

Number 93: creative, in architecture and landscaping. Non commitment

Number 94: practical humanitarian, not comfortable with travel, and dislikes changes.

Number 95: humanitarian, is impractical, dreamer. loves travel and change.

Number 96: loving nature self-sacrificing focused on community family, friends, and relations.

Number 97: sensitive. quiet worker and loves to read.

Number 98: idealist, shows emotions. not easily understood by others.

Number 99: artistic genius. often misunderstood, victim of gossip, brings jealousy possessiveness to relationships and friendship.

# CHAPTER 33

## Numerology

Know About Your Self
Through Numerology

READ WHAT YOUR BIRTH NO HAS TO SAY ABOUT YOU

COMPATIBILITY WITH OTHER NUMBERS

Natives Ruled By Number 1

People born with various numbers, when we stand to applying numerology compatibility, us to find out who will be helpful to them in all their dealings. If you are born on 1st, 10th, 19th or 28th dates, your ruling number is 1. Natives who are governed by 1, with get help from people who are of 4, and 2 number persons of 7 as their number will also help them. Help and joint venture Differ In Numerology Compatibility. Please note help you from 8 persons will be good solid and long standing. There is no dispute or conflict with numerology compatibility for 1 and 8, But their marriage, love or joint venture in business, politics, or board meetings, will not be successful, as these persons will have opposite views on most matters and will not see eye to eye. Their vibrations oppose each other.

COMPATIBILITY
Natives Ruled By Number 2

If your birth day is 2nd, 11th, 20th or 29th, your number is 2. You will get help from natives ruled by 7. But people with 2 as number people are unreliable for you because, they may do you both good and bad. You can choose persons of 1, 3, 4, and 8, number person who will be help you and do good for you. If may become difficult for number 7 people to find out the right companion or partner for them for any help or assistance.

COMPATIBILITY
Natives Ruled By Number 3

If you are born on 3rd, 12th, 21st, or 30th. Your Number is 3.

Persons ruled by 2 and 9 will be quite helpful. But you need to avoid people ruled by 5 and 6. You should also avoid Number 7 and Number 8 people They may not be helpful, fruitful and useful.

COMPATIBILITY
Natives Ruled By Number 4

If you are born on 4th, 13th, 22nd, or 31st, your Number is 4. You tend to get help is from persons whose have numbers 1 or 8. Slight help can be expected from the 4 and 2. But, from people with number 8 you will receive unexpected favors.

COMPATIBILITY
Natives Ruled By Number 5

If you are born on 5th, 14th, or 23th, your day number is 5. You seem to be the most fortunate and lucky person as compared to others. You ought to get help from all sides and corners. All the persons from 1 to 9, will be glad to help you.

COMPATIBILITY
Natives Ruled By Number 6

If you are born on 6th, 15th, or 24th your number is 6. As per symmetrical and multiple laws of numerology compatibility, you tend to get help from persons of 3, 6, and 9. You can expect to get excellent and extra ordinary help from number 3 natives also.

COMPATIBILITY
Natives Ruled By Number 7

If you are born on 7th, 16th, and 25th your number is 7. You would get help from natives ruled by 2, 7, 1, and 4. You can know your compatibility to your number with regards to the circle of your friends to know who comes under these numbers to assist you and help you in the event of crisis.

COMPATIBILITY
Natives Ruled By Number 8

If you are born on 8th, 17th, or 26th, you are ruled by number 8. You ought to get help only from the persons ruled by 1 and 4. You can also expect help from persons ruled by 8. But, this is a bit on lower side.

COMPATIBILITY
Natives Ruled By Number 9

If you are born on 9th, 18th, or 27th, your number is 9. Getting to apply numerology compatibility persons ruled by 3, 5, 6, and 9 would be helpful to you. But Persons ruled by 2 could harm you even if they try to assist and help you.

# CHAPTER 34

## Numerology

Know About Your Self
Through Numerology

READ WHAT YOUR BIRTH NO 10 HAS TO SAY ABOUT YOU

RELATIONSHIP

Relationship between Numbers, Alphabets and Planets,

In Numerology you can visualize a close Relationship between Numbers, Alphabets and Planets. The above all three shower immense vibrations. When these are in harmony, they are very lucky for you. Below is a Table of Numbers Alphabets and Planets. Each Planet vibrates in Harmony with its Number. And its Alphabets.

They are represented by these Numbers.

| Planet | Number | Alphabet |
|---|---|---|
| Sun | 1 | A J S |
| Moon | 2 | B K T |
| Jupiter | 3 | C L U |
| Rahu, Uranus | 4 | D M V |
| Mercury | 5 | E N W |
| Venus | 6 | F O X |
| Ketu Neptune | 7 | G P Y |
| Saturn | 8 | H Q Z |
| Mars | 9 | I R |

# CHAPTER 35

# Numerology

Know About Your Self
Through Numerology

READ WHAT YOUR BIRTH NO HAS TO SAY ABOUT YOU

NUMEROLOGY AND PLANETS

## Number Ruled by Planet
## Sun

If you are born on the 1st, 10th, 19th, and 28th, of any month, the total when added of your birth number it becomes 1

You are ruled by Planet Sun.

It is said that you will be bold honest and straight forward and will order, control and influence all. You are strong diligent, and you work very hard to be successful. You are best situated for head of Religion, Political Leader, and good administrator.

This number also indicates that you can shine well in teaching astrology politics, medicine, and fine arts. You shy away from cheating and fraud and deceit. You would work hard to become a famous leader. At times you can become arrogant and proud and would blow your own trumpet, claim to be number one and often make false promises, and thus face failures. By this you generate enemies.

If you are a fairer sex or a lady, you appear to be more grown up. You may get eye sight and may need to wear spectaculars in life soon. After 45, you may be a victim of hyper tension or heart disease or some chest ailments.

## NUMEROLOGY AND PLANETS

# Number Ruled by Planet
# MOON

If you are born on the 2nd, 11th, 20th, and 29th, of any month the total when added of your birth number becomes 2 you are ruled by the planet Moon.

This number ruled by moon influences your, thoughts, mind and imagination. Like water waves, you may have different moods of elevation and depression.

This tends to control your imagination, and allows you to become a great scholar. When your imagination runs out of control or amok, you seek to lose your head, and you wake up as a Lunatic or a mentally depressed person.

You could have a wavering temperament. In business, You toil and build the important toe or line of someone else than to work for your own profits. You find it to be an easy task to do this.

Since this planet Moon derives its light from the Sun. You too ought to shine in borrowed brightness and glory. As planet Moon do not show its one side to Earth. Similarly, you tend to hide your dark side from the public vision.

This planet shows that you are swayed by negative thoughts and suspicion. You show a rough exterior side to others. On the reverse side you are soft in your nature, like a cool glow of moon light. When someone becomes offensive against you, you are baffled and rattled. You try to compromise. But if someone is under your authority, you enslave them, terrorize them, and extract work from them.

At some point of time if some of your subordinate retaliates your emotions, you tend to become irritated and make you to surrender. This also makes you nurse fears about everyone and you do like to trust others. You like to do all by yourself. Numerology Meanings for No. 2 also reveal that, if you trust some persons, you fall for their flattery, and you get badly cheated. This is why, you have to be careful in your choice of friends. Assess well before choosing.

## NUMEROLOGY AND PLANETS

# Number Ruled by Planet
# JUPITER

If you are born on the 3rd, 12th, 21st, and 30th, of any month, the total when added of your birth number becomes 3 you are ruled by the planet Jupiter.

In Numerology, number 3 stands for Jupiter. He is named as Guru of Devtas in Heaven. The planet Jupiter is also the Lord of signs Sagittarius and Pisces in the zodiac signs .

Since planet Jupiter rules Number3. It donates and signifies Wisdom Knowledge, Selflessness Sacrifice, and Service.

This number 3 and the planet ruling it makes you honest, hardworking and intelligent. You expect discipline from your colleagues and subordinates and also adhere to and obey your superiors implicitly. In spite being a tough exterior, you are not hard hearted. You only do what is reasonable for you and as per your conscience. You do not mind to help others, even without even thinking of any returns.

This number and the influence of this planet makes you orthodox. You follow your own culture and religion. You do not like to change your ways of life as per social norms. But you shy away from asking for help on the contrary you would like to help others. Your self-respect prevents you from doing that. This name umber and planet makes you good and great in nature and you may appear to be proud superficially. The name number also get you into altruistic deeds. You attain high positions in politics, by your own efforts and hard work. As such you are considered to be a lucky chap. If anything is to come to you it comes only after your sincere hard work.

This number imparts you rise and promotion only through gradual rise step by step. You would not t desire for anything which you cannot perform. You most of the time try to remain content with whatever comes to you in the course of your life, by sincere hard and honest work.

With this ruling number, you are of two types. One with a good self-confidence, and the other without weak and timid. If you are the first type, you are bold, confident in what you do. You fight for what is right and justified, neglecting and unmindful of your oppositions. You have a self—scarifying nature and you would not mind scarifying for your country in the need of any crises and you would be ready to any suffering and personal loss.

Now if you happen to be of the second type, you would obey your elders and remain quiet. You work only for you and your family. Even if you do something good, you would justify yourself to be satisfied with a name, but may not get and publicity and become famous.

The added quality of this number is that it makes you the strong pillars of post in offices, institutions and in government departments. You would fill all the important government positions to serve officers, ministers and organizations. This number and planet also make you to shy away from earning a bad name. You stand for high regard and prestige. You are not interested to start or run a big institution. On the contrary you would like to work gladly for those who offer you good respect and service.

On the reverse side of it if your name number 3 gets weakened you turn out to be lazy, fond of vices gambling and do all unjust things. You become sensual, borrow funds, and fail to return, indulge in unlawful activities and even court imprisonment. Therefore, it is important to correct your name with positive vibrations of a new name by an expert.

## NUMEROLOGY AND PLANETS

# Number Ruled by Planet
# RAHU

If you are born on the 4th, 13th, 22nd, or 31st., of any month, you are ruled by No. 4. You are ruled by Planet Rahu.

With this number and planet you become the a well-known person and people take you as a well-judged and well Informed person, well known, and a Source for Information, as a ready reckoner and an intelligent person.

You are a knowledgeable person who is fond of, collecting information about all walks of life and is always busy. You mostly represent a circle. You can cause changes in social circle, and your society. It is often your opinion which counts as the main public opinion.

Your name is well known in social circles. You are like and your name is on the lips of every one, as an authority, when somebody needs any information. You have the power of tongue to express, or gift of the gab or bridge. Your this number rules, your Intellect. You can cause and effect social revolutions. You make reformation and social changes by your speech and great literary writings. You are always seen busy talking to someone, or helping the others.

This makes you gather latest information on all subjects. You are the trusted source of information, on a wide range of subjects. We can see you in the street corners, restaurants, clubs and press meets. Your number represents The planet Earth. Its presiding lord is Ganesha.

Therefore, you happen to sharp and intelligent, soft spoken and pleasant. You are acquainted with almost everything and everyone. You have a wide range of friends. Your name makes you to be an authoritative person and your opinions cross others with the alternate views, If you are trying to be adamant, you also acquire secret enmity among your friend circles.

Also if you name and nature is in affliction you possess the power to change this nature well in time, to become amiable to all. You can win almost all friends and influence people. But you tend to keep only surface friendship with the ost, and maintain only a few close and sincere friends.

You are good in philosophy, literature, mythologies, research and religion. You keep on acquiring knowledge on a wider range of topics. This number makes you not so keen on becoming famous. You would like to fully enjoy life and are very much careful about your diet like your food and drinks. You are the one who asks for special medicines and tonics to improve your health.

On the positive side of it you are soft in nature. You are full of emotions and are easily hurt. But, you forget it quickly to get along well. Money does not come to you that easy.

You struggle for your earnings. But you enjoy spending money. You take pleasure in shopping for the latest gadgets in the and new electronics items in the market. You feel happy and get pleasure in keeping your house and drawing room very attractive.

You specially amaze your friends with your rare collections of different items. You are fond of games and you want to enjoy life to its fullest. During your old age, you do researches on Vedas, and philosophical literature. In your life, you think well, to indulge in those activities, which brings good wealth for you.

On the negative side of it your number is not considered and favored to be a good number and is often said that it is not good to have your name number as 4. If you have 4 as the day number and 8 as your life number, you will face lots of complications. It is always better for you to correct your name, by some expert fellow who can measure the vibrations of the number, and get the effect to a good change.

## NUMEROLOGY AND PLANETS

# Number Ruled by Planet
# MERCURY

If you are born on the 5th, 14th, and 23rd, of any month, be sure that you are ruled by 5 and Planet is Mercury. You are ruled by Planet Mercury.

If you re ruled by No. 5 and planet Mercury you often take daring risks, consider nothing as impossible to achieve. Your Intellect works with tremendous Speed, and you become quite popular and successful in a short span of time. You quickly think of new methods and ideas, for which others take months. You work so well and often take the lead for the rapid modern developments in our scientific life. You consider the whole world lags behind you. As you are fond of new business ventures and you do not get scared or are afraid of failures. You are lucky and successful and are liked by masses. Even If your day number is not 5 but your main number is 5, you start your life as per your day number; with the result you will be very popular in your later life. At times you can also be notorious, vagabond and non-reliable.

Your No. 5 gives you special powers of special attraction. Successful businessmen know this and change their business names to No. 5, in order to be successful. You can never fail. You fight back and win which makes you to constantly like changes and get into new enterprises. You are quite bored by routine.

Your spouse need to understand this secret of yours numerology. This number also ensures your business success. You can do any kind of business successfully. You think of quick tricky and novel ways of making money. If you fail it becomes the stepping stone for your next big venture. You also like to earn well and spend well. If your this number is well placed in your birth chart and exalted, then, you achieve great name and fame. You perform miraculous and memorable things. You invent new ideas, new ways of marketing and new methods. Your number 5 warns that you have to be careful with your secrets. You simply cannot hide anything from others and this being your weakness you tend to lose all that is gained.

Your number five makes you easily to fall in love. It is instant love and out of passion rather than any reason. Changing everything is your passion and you love to change and this leads you to change your love quite often. You may end up in serious trouble for you.

Natives with ruling numbers 9, 18, and 27 attract you much. They would rule over you in the long run. Thus you need to make a wise choice. Persons ruled by No. 5, are not blessed to get children easily. If both husband and wife have the same number and are ruled by No. 5, then the question of issues is delayed or at times denied. It is better for them to try from early stages. If your this number happens to be afflicted you lead a life of telling lies by trickery and cheating others with false and fraudulent methods. You mishandle public funds. To avoid all this, you must correct your names with accurate vibrations by a good numerologist.

## NUMEROLOGY AND PLANETS

# Number Ruled by Planet
# VENUS

If you are born on the 6th, 15th, and 24th, of any month, the total when added of your birth number becomes 6you are ruled by the planet Venus.

You would attain greatness in you gradually and this will transform your life to a status of comforts and luxury. No. 6 stands for Planet Venus this gives you an award to become are attractive, popular, and loved by all. This number will also make you to be fond of dance and music drama and theatre.

This loving number enriches you to dominate and rule over others. You would be surrounded by servants this will make you to lead a luxurious life. You tend to be gifted with name, fame, and riches. This number will also make you to love all attractive things. You will love beautiful things by nature and you will consider this life is to be fully enjoyable. You want to enjoy every moment and pleasure of your life. You possess a special quality to extract work from others in order to achieve your goals. And you work very hard, to make money.

This number and planetary influence makes you to become a great and good leader, and you would easily govern to rule experts, even though you do not have their knowledge.

You are helped by others to come up in your life. This also makes you excel in mantra, and all mystical sciences. You would get help from others, but you do not always reciprocate. You make false promises, and fail to keep them. You do not indulge in any superficial schemes and are always careful about your money and bank balance.

Number six makes you to give less and take more from others who serve you. Even if you make a go at others, there will be a money motive behind that. You will calculate profits and then only start anything. This number makes you to decorate your home with attractive things. And this makes you to spend money on costly and beautiful things. You love to be surrounded by opposite sex. Your love for ornaments and attraction for beauty makes you to lead a luxurious life.

You are a sweet-tongued person and by way of this nature you accumulate wealth using others method help and their talents, just to make your life look beautiful. Natives with 6 as their number are born lucky. They are very attractive, which makes others like you.

You are talented in your persistence and you achieve success. You would like to purchase success at any price thus you would enjoy others work and sacrifice. You are gifted with great riches and wealth. You tend live in a grand luxury.

If this number is in affliction it makes you to become a cheater. You cheat others very cunning and boldly. People known to you often get themselves cheated by you. You speak sweet and attractive words to delude and cheat them.

This number when it is in powerful condition and the planet Venus influences you in a positive manner you enter the fields of medicine, religion, in all mystic sciences like mantras and tantras and false remedies, about which yourself may not know anything. But you pretend to possess the a deep knowledge of everything. Thus you speak lies, to cheat others and make a living for yourself. You are not afraid of failures. You boldly try and try again to achieve great success.

## NUMEROLOGY AND PLANETS

# Number Ruled by Planet
# Ketu Neptune

If your are born on 7, 16, or 25 in any month, you are ruled by Number 7. total when added to your birth number it becomes 7 which indicates you are Ruled by Planet Ketu, Neptune

This number and planet makes you a saint a religious person and above all a philosopher. As far as your luck of natives of number seven is concerned, they lack to be lucky, in spite of their mental caliber and immense knowledge. If at all they become successful it is only after a lot of extreme hard work, struggle and hardships. Success eludes you in all your endeavors.

Many persons fail and end up doing small jobs and many others live with unfulfilled wishes desires and ambitions. Your ambitions tend to be more successful than your works of personal gain. You are bound to succeed, only if you work for others, than for your own profit.

The number seven persons have great powers of the mind and intellect. Since this number is ruled by Ketu which is a signification for wisdom. The 7 born are usually religious and inclined to be great thinkers and philosophers. On the positive side natives with number seven as their number are gifted with greater will power. Because of high mental energy, they talk less and speak in silence. However they can be good leaders but poor followers.

Such natives are often moody even with close persons. They easily become short tempered. Hence, they have few friends and do not properly enjoy their marital life. You tend to live separately or opt for divorce. The seven born fairer sex are seldom graced by beauty. Often their feminine charm is missing. They too find marriage bit difficult and feel unhappy in their married lives.

## NUMEROLOGY AND PLANETS

# Number Ruled by Planet
# SATURN

Saturn And No. 8

In Name Numerology, No. 8 stands for Planet Saturn total when added to your birth number it becomes 8 which indicates that you are ruled by Planet Saturn.

Be sure that you are ruled by number 8 if you face too many obstacles, often meet with accidents, Don't feel unlucky, it may be effect of Saturn.

When this number is well placed in your birth chart or when it is exalted it makes you to become a saint, a religious follower. But if it happens to get afflicted, it makes you to commit crimes. Also if your Life number alone is 8, you will get the traits and qualities of No. 8 in due course of your life, and may undergo many sufferings your early days throughout your life. This number leads to you to face a lot of obstacles, which you may suffer from your childhood. You get small and little things, only after great struggles. You meet with many unexpected failures, accidents, and rejections. You would have too many risks even when you hold high positions.

When this gets into purity, you get the power to understand the scriptures. You are filled with compassion, love, and mercy. You sacrifice for the poor and the sick and will work for the down trodden. You spend your life in serving the poor and the sick. You get into religious teachings. You are eager to strike with God.

This number tends to makes you appear nice and clean. But from inside, you are see things with rage and thoughts of revenge. You revel in plans of rape fraud cheating, blackmails, murder and enter into the trade of counterfeit currencies. This also drives you to commit crimes and fill the prisons. But the same time, though you harbor such thoughts, but you lack the courage to do such acts. The planet Saturn that rules your number reveals that he stands for justice and administers it without fear or favor. He weighs your past deeds and punishes you and you get the deserved fruits accordingly.

These holy texts written on name numerology describe the bad luck of No. 8, but fails as how to escape from its evil effects. Intensive researchers have written that by changing names, the evil and bad effects for such persons are reduced to mere small events.

It has been said and told that if you modify your name number as to be 5 you would be buried from all evil effects of the bad planetary influence of this planet Saturn. Number 5 adds the power of good luck to you. Therefore, whatever are your sufferings with number 8, and if you have a proper name change in the tune and vibrations of No. 5, you are sure to escape from bad luck and ill effects. Hence with the help of an expert you need to change your name in the proper vibration of No. 5 that suits you.

## NUMEROLOGY AND PLANETS

# Number Ruled by Planet
# Mars

Mars and No. 9

If your number falls on the 9th, 18th, and 27th, of any month, you are ruled by 9 and Planet Mars. This number when added happens to be 9 you can confirm it that you are ruled by this number and planet only. Number nine is ruled by Mars.

Your number 9 is the highest in the series from 1 to 9. When multiplied to any number by this number 9, it bounces back to 9. And per this you will attain to the status as shown by 9 and if your number is single nine, you develop the qualities for 9 only. When you a fight for a cause, or rebel against an oppression, and fight for your country, you are ruled by Number nine.

You shine as a lawyer, chemist, doctor or a technician. This is the number that of a person born as a man who walks intelligently, on a road full of blood spots and stains, not seeing the danger below him. It tells you that your life is covered with dangers and accidents. This number also makes you a born fighter. You will everything without any fear and this makes you an embodiment of courage.

This number fills your life with struggles. You happen to struggle with oppression, cruelty and authority and poverty. You would be fitted with the skills of the plumber, the machinist, the carpenter, the farmer, the doctor and the scientist or an engineer. You fight against the old and create a new order. You construct buildings, dams, and bridges. You also destroy them with bombs, in an emergency, or during war. You are the back bone of any civilization or any generation.

This number and planet generates love your country and are also in love your with your society which in turn makes you to help your fellow citizens. You would sacrifice everything for your nation. You also tend to fight for the rights and freedom of your fellow countrymen.

This number also makes you join the army, navy, or the air force. For most, you try to become a police officer. You like to handle the fire arms, machine guns, and bombs without any fear. You obey rules and you also demand obedience. You fight for your honor. You sacrifice your life for your country. You are blessed with sharp intellect. You appear cool in any crisis. You hide your feelings. But you plan secretly to defeat your enemies. You weigh all the pros and cons and strike to win and get it without much difficulty.

Many of you happen to become scholars and philosophers and intellectuals. This also makes you fit to become an intelligent leader and a good politician. When this number happens to be afflicted or is less lucky you tend betray your emotions and engage in quarrels. You generate enemies in this manner and waste your energy.

If your number is affected by evils, it gives you a feeling of pride. You are charged with greed and jealousy. You brood on your weaknesses and on your enemies. You burst with anger. You become a nasty street fighter.

You are good at rare inventions. This fact gives you deep insights into chemistry and medicine. You exhibit your special powers, when your number is in exalting position. Be warned that you should not be polluted by bad associations of No. 2, 4, 7 or 8. When 9 is afflicted by your day number or name number, you are rude. You acquire bad traits and evil habits. When 9 is afflicted, you turn arrogant and commanding. You dictate terms. You are filled with lust. You get addicted to drugs and alcohol. You take pleasure in torturing and hurting others.

You can have your name organized and you should not have your name in Numbers matching the twos sevens or eights. If at all that is so in such situations, that you must correct your number 9 numerology by making your name vibrate in perfect harmony with your day and life numbers. Get it rectified and corrected by an expert numerologist, who can measure your name vibrations. Your number also attracts people to come forward to help you.

A single person like you will not make the most and you cannot be built without the helps from persons known to you and in your circle. You have people, all around and you only need to find them to succeed. Hence you need to apply your numerology compatibility to choose for best help and enlist their support you will succeed to be a winner.

# CHAPTER 36

## Numerology

Know About Your Self
Through Numerology

READ WHAT YOUR BIRTH NO HAS TO SAY ABOUT YOU

GEMS AND STONES
FOR ALL NUMBERS

Gem Stone for No. 1

The best suited stone or gem according to numerology for number one is Ruby. It enhances your fortune or your luck powerfully. Alternately you can also use yellow sapphire and Topaz. These would help improve your health and give you success in your actions, deeds and in your life.

We could find that these gems, helps in promoting healthy growth in our young sons and daughters. As an grown up person, you could wear Ruby or yellow sapphire. Both are fine for you. You have to wear it in your right hand in ring finger made in gold ring.

## Gem Stone for No. 2

The best suited stone or gem according to numerology for number two is Pearl. It enhances your fortune or your luck abundantly. Alternately you can also use Jade, Moon stone, and Tiger's Eye. These would help improve your health and give you success in your actions, deeds in your life.

All are fine for you. You have to wear it in your right hand in smallest finger made in silver ring. Jade has a particular medical use. It relieves your stomach disorders. The Tigers Eye is good for your children.

## Gems for No. 3

The best suited stone or gem according to numerology for number three is Amethyst. Amethyst is of a violet color. There are many benefits. It enhances your luck abundantly. Alternately known for its anti-drunkenness properties, it greatly powers you up in your decisions.

It prevents you forever from becoming over intoxicated. These would help improve your health and give you success in your actions, deeds in your life. You can also use yellow sapphire with a golden hue. It is also highly favorable for you. It enhances your luck and worldly success. You must were your gem in your left hand, in your ring finger, studding it over gold.

## Gems for no. 4

The best suited stone or gem according to numerology for number Four is Garnet.. There are many benefits. It enhances your luck abundantly. The next choice is blue sapphire. Select it with the blue light color. Alternatively opal can also be used.

## Gems for No. 5

The best suited stone or gem according to numerology for number Five is, Diamond. It should be highly of good quality and have the specification and be genuinely pure. It should be seen that it need to shine with the glow of the light. Zircon can be used as an alternate gem.

## Gems for No. 6

The best suited stone or gem according to numerology for number six is Emerald. Circular or opal size structure should be taken. It powers mental strength, self-confidence, and immense happiness. It should be a flawless piece having some luster.

## Gems for No.7

The best suited stone or gem according to numerology for number seven is Cat's Eye. There are many benefits. It enhances your fortune and makes you very strong.

## Gems for Number 8

The best suited stone or gem according to numerology for number eight is Blue Sapphire. It can be tested, put a piece of blue sapphire in a glass of milk and if the there is a bluish layer than it is a good gem to be worn. High quality Sapphire showers good luck.

## Gems for number 9

The best suited stone or gem according to numerology for number nine is Coral. It comes from the deep seas from the coral rocks, created by coral making insects. It removes blood related diseases and showers immense Luck. It gives you victory over your enemies. It bestows health and riches.

# CHAPTER 37

## Numerology

Know About Your Self
Through Numerology

READ WHAT YOUR BIRTH NO HAS TO SAY ABOUT YOU

The Letters of Your Name and Numerology
FOR ALL NUMBERS

**W**hen analyzing your own name, it's important to know that in Numerology, each letter in your name has a specific meaning and a number corresponding to it, and the influence that letter has on you. Someone who has changed the first vowel in their name for some reason, indicates a person who was uncomfortable and is now fine after changing his name letter to the compatibility of its number with his name. Here is a brief description as to what your name alphabets means in terms of numerology to you.

They are from A to Z we describe the same as follows:

The specific meaning of letter A in Your Name

You are a natural leader have some fine ambitious and a free thinking personality. If someone pressurizes you and makes you to change your mind you straight away appose him.

The specific meaning of letter B in Your Name

You are sensitive but still manage to be compassionate and personable and compassionate. In order to be happy you always desire to be at peace. Although you are very sincere and loyal, you seek to keep an open mind and think for yourself more often than others.

The specific meaning of letter C in Your Name

You have a strong instinct and you work whole heartedly in any project. You express yourself freely with the result you are also very outspoken and upbeat. You have a strong courage to face any eventuality.

The specific meaning of letter D in Your Name

You need not be too stubborn as you are master in of getting the things done. Your sense of determination is strong. You sparkle under pressure and can get things quickly. You are grounded and pragmatic.

The specific meaning of letter E in Your Name

You love to have freedom. You believe strongly in parting and outings. You are the one who cannot be easily fooled. You can see a situation from many different angles.

The specific meaning of letter F in Your Name

You are good host, self-sacrificing and very easy to get along with. Your warmness shows in how easily you're able to take on other peoples grieve. Be careful not to indulge in positions where you're not comfortable, and try not to let other people's worries and problems drag you down.

The specific meaning of letter G in Your Name

You are an active person with the caliber to make things happen. You have a strong vision, and this could help you financially in the long run. You need to stand on your feet, even though you prefer to be very organized. At times you may feel bit to psychic. You may even feel psychic sometimes.

The specific meaning of letter H in Your Name

You have a strong vision to manipulate, also tend to make a lot of money and lose it fast. You may be ok with it in the long run. Your creativity will help you well. You would prefer to be alone. You would like to spend more time in outings and parties rather than fighting with others.

The specific meaning of letter I in Your Name

You are a compassionate artistic and a creative person who feels things deeply and have a great eye for everything. Make sure you have a nice balance and have the correct direction otherwise you might suffer from depression.

The specific meaning of letter J in Your Name

J spells the meaning in you that you are a well-balanced person. You are all about balancing the scales. You make an extra ordinary friend and you do your to work hard and try your best to make sure everyone is happy and comfortable. You need to motivate yourself to tap into natural talents.

The specific meaning of letter K in Your Name

You are an entertainer and it all about enlightenment with you. You get motivated and rely heavily on your skill to make good decisions. You are also a force to be reckoned with. Be careful of excitement or depression, because you tend to be highly effected.

The specific meaning of letter L in Your Name

You are very brainy, and tend experience life. But you should not allow this experience to make you arrogant. You have the qualities to be kind-hearted, honest and generous. Though you are quite fond of travel, you should always be careful during times of excitement and depression. You must maintain and equal balance.

The specific meaning of letter M in Your Name

You are fond of doing excess work and possess a high quantity of energy, to do extra work and you don't need much rest or sleep and are very healthy. You also really like to be a homebody, however, and need a steady financial base in order to feel secure. Also make sure your drive doesn't make you impatient with other people.

The specific meaning of letter N in Your Name

You seem to be creative, original. You are also strong-willed and you have strong opinions to match with the people of your interest. You are organized in your life, with would like your share of romantic meetings.

The specific meaning of letter O in Your Name

Your moral is high and your spiritual believe is quite strong as is your will. You would like to make laws and rules, you are also sensitive and take all things very deeply. You must avoid being jealous might be a problem for you. Be careful not to and suspicious.

The specific meaning of letter P in Your Name

You are very intelligent possess immense knowledge, You are the center of attraction and People get great first impressions from you, but you can also seem keep distant from them. Although you have great sense to be patient but at times you can be extremely short tempered and impatient. Make sure to let this go, be more generous with the growing time.

The specific meaning of letter Q in Your Name

You are a magnet of collecting immense money, but your intolerance and instability can lead to financial downfalls. You are a born leader with a great power to preside, but on a personal level, you're a tough nut to crack. People find you mysterious and may gossip frequently about you.

The specific meaning of letter R in Your Name

You take things very strongly and you enrich the power of your but do not image it outwardly. You are work alcoholic and can do your job with high energy. You need to make sure to keep a balance and work well with others, even though you are prone to this nature.

The specific meaning of letter S in Your Name

You need to make sure that you are taking every decision very carefully. You being real charmer, a sense of warmth and devotion is being inherited but this can lead to overly dramatic situations and you may be confronted with many emotional ups and downs.

The specific meaning of letter T in Your Name

As you are in often seen tackling with new and exciting projects. You would like to move in fast lane but you must be reminded by yourself to slow down at bit. Being aggressive in your relationships. you appearance should be in check, and not too sensitive.

The specific meaning of letter U in Your Name

You are prone to a policy of give and take and would like to lead this kind of life. You might gain a lot, only to lose it, but neither less will always break even. Power yourself to think faster on your feet and then commit wholeheartedly to involved with anything. You need to guide your instinct and creativity. You look glamorous in awkward situations too will show your positive temperament.

The specific meaning of letter V in Your Name

You are a pillar and you have great intuition. At times you may even feel bit psychic. Having a strong imagination, it may be hard to separate fact from fiction. You have high aimed goals and the will to bring them into reality. Use your efficiency, but be careful not to be too centered, there lies the real danger.

The specific meaning of letter W in Your Name

You think from your inner heart and you have a great sense of a purpose. You being an active person, you like to be involved in as many activities. Your mystical magic means you surround yourself with interesting people, because you have the powers of excellent conversation. You are advised to take full advantage of your own creative.

The specific meaning of letter X in Your Name

You have the quality of being creative, sensual person who mix up with people easily and gathers important information like a sponge. Be careful that this enthusiasm and passion doesn't make you too passionate in sexual matters. You can also be moody and have to be careful to avoid addictions.

The specific meaning of letter Y in Your Name

You come across to be self-reserved person even though you may love to be free and your ambition and courage make you naturally independent, even though. You need to avoid being too slow in making decisions or else you would lose all the profits that you have gained.

The specific meaning of letter Z in Your Name

You possess magical and mystical and you usual take the sunny side of the street, to say that you have high standards of living. You balance this out with common sense and understanding. You are wise and quick on your feet, but should not to be impatient or impulsive.

# CHAPTER 38

## Numerology

Know About Your Self
Through Numerology

READ WHAT YOUR BIRTH NO HAS TO SAY ABOUT YOU

BRIEF DISCRIPTION OF YOUR NUMBERS
FOR ALL NUMBERS

Number 1—Initiative, independence, forcefulness
(a masculine number).

Number 2—Tact, diplomacy, attention to details
(a feminine number).

Number 3—Self-expression, ambition, spirituality, luck, easy
success.

Number 4—Labor, material, routine work—little paid
compensation, unlucky.

Number 5—Inventive genius, imagination, charm, restlessness,
adventurous.

Number 6—Tenacity, conscientiousness, achievement by
working with others, domestic.

Number 7—Mysticism, isolation, poets and dreamers; misunderstood by co-workers or companions.

Number 8—Reason, judgment, financial success, organization.

Number 9—Sympathy, generosity, dramatic, artistic talent (higher octave—teacher, master).

## Planets and Numbers

There are many Planets in our System on which all calculations are based. Each planet rules a particular sign and has individual characteristic, vibration, trait that influences the person born under it. Each planet is given a number. The Nine Planets, with Corresponding Numbers and, their Zodiac signs are:

The sun and the moon are the only two planets having 'double numbers'. The sun and Uranus are interrelated and so is the moon and Neptune. There is a strong attraction between numbers 1-4 and 2-7 and these four numbers are compatible with each other.

Numbers 7 and 4 were allotted to the moon and the sun until Neptune and Uranus were discovered. Presently, number 4 is the number of planet Uranus or Rahu

| PLANET | RULES NUMBER | ZODIAC SIGNs |
|---|---|---|
| Mars | 9 | Aries |
| Venus | 6 | Taurus |
| Mercury | 5 | Gemini |
| Moon | 2, 7 | Cancer |
| Sun | 1, 4 | Leo |
| Mercury | 5 | Virgo |
| Venus | 6 | Libra |
| Mars | 9 | Scorpio |
| Jupiter | 3 | Sagittarius |
| Saturn | 8 | Capricorn Aquarius |
| Jupiter | 3 | Pisces |

## THE END

OUR FIRST PUBLICATION
ON SALE IS
'MICROSCOPY OF ASTROLOGY'

ORDERS FOR BOOKS CAN BE PLACED AT:

orders.india@partridgepublishing.com

channelsales@authorsolutions.com

AND AT OUR CONTACT ADDRESS:
PLEASE SEND YOUR QUERIES TO:

BALDEV BHATIA
CONSULTANT-NUMEROLOGY-ASTROLOGY
C-63, FIRST FLOOR
MALVIYA NAGAR
NEW DELHI-110017
INDIA

TEL NO 91 9810075249
TEL NO 91 1126686856
TEL NO 91 7503280786
TEL NO 91 7702735880

MAIL US AT:
baldevbhatia@yahoo.com

# OUR MOST SOUGHT WEB SITES:

HTTP://WWW.ASTROLOGYBB.COM
HTTP://WWW.BBASTROLOGY.COM
HTTP://WWW.BALDEVBHATIA.COM
HTTP://WWW.BALDEVBHATIA.US
HTTP://WWW.BALDEVBHATIA.ORG
HTTP://WWW.BALDEVBHATIA.INFO
HTTP://WWW.BALDEVBHATIA.NET
HTTP://WWW.BALDEVBHATIA.BIZ
HTTP://WWW.BALDEVBHATIA.IN
HTTP://WWW.MICROSCOPYOFASTROLOGY.COM


SPECIAL NOTE
FROM THE AUTHOR BALDEV BHATIA

THANK YOU FOR READING MY BOOK
MY SINCERE PRAYERS

FOR ALL MY READERS
"GOD BLESS YOU ALL"

"ANY ONE WHO READS AND KEEPS THIS BOOK AS HOLY
MANUSCRIPT,GOD IS SURE TO BLESS HIM, WITH ALL THE
PEACE, HAPPINESS, WEALTH, HEALTH AND PROSPERITY
OF THIS UNIVERSE"

Baldev Bhatia